The Ocean

Exploring Interactions Beneath the Waves

DEVELOPED IN COOPERATION
WITH

THE THOMAS H. KEAN NEW JERSEY STATE AQUARIUM AT CAMDEN
CAMDEN, NEW JERSEY

Copyright © 1995 by Scholastic Inc.   All rights reserved. Published by Scholastic Inc.   Printed in the U.S.A.
ISBN 0-590-27666-2
2 3 4 5 6 7 8 9 10   09   01 00 99 98 97 96 95

EARTH, WITHIN THE UNIVERSE, IS CONSTANTLY CHANGING.

The Ocean

The ocean is one global body of water with unique characteristics and resources.

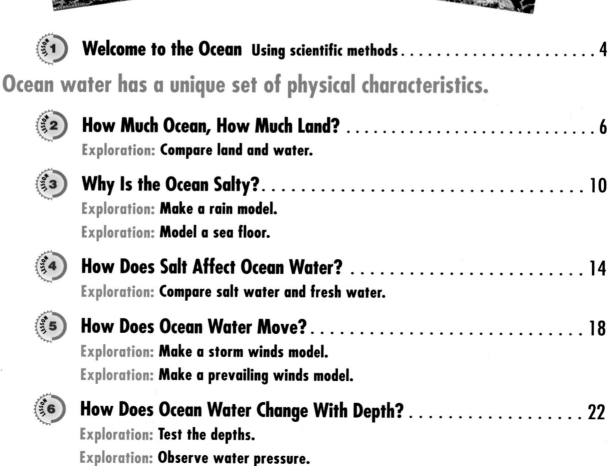

The ocean's environments provide a wide range of conditions that allow for a great diversity of life.

The ocean affects humans, and human activities affect the ocean.

Think Tank: Living Under Water Exploration Lab

Welcome to the Ocean

It's big. It's blue. It's mysterious. Many parts of it haven't ever been seen by human eyes.

The ocean has always been a place of mystery for people. Stories of sea monsters terrified sailors for centuries, and people believed that boats sailing too far out to sea would fall off the edge of the planet. Even today, people are amazed by stories of fierce sharks and giant octopuses.

What's the real story of the ocean? You're about to find out.

What do you know about the ocean?

Even if you don't live close to the ocean, you probably already know some things about it. If you live near a coast, you probably know quite a lot. Work with your class to make a list of what you already know.

What do you want to know?

Make a second list with the rest of your class. This time, list questions you have about the ocean. You could start your list with a question about one of the pictures: Are octopuses really dangerous?

How will you find out?

As you work in teams to do the hands-on explorations in this unit, you'll discover many of the answers to your questions. You'll also share information discovered by other teams in your class, and by other scientists.

Using scientific methods:

Take a close look at the table of contents. Each lesson title is a problem you're going to solve. Each problem you solve will help you solve the ones that come after it. In each exploration lesson, you and your class will use scientific methods to solve each problem:

• You'll make a *hypothesis*—a prediction—about possible answers to the problem.

• You'll do a *hands-on exploration*—sometimes two of them—that will help you test your hypothesis.

• You'll *record data* you collect.

• You'll *draw conclusions* from your data.

• You'll *compare* your conclusions to those of other teams in your class.

• You'll *apply* your conclusions to your own life.

The Video Field Trip will help you get started. You're going to be taken to the scene of a mystery. Witnesses to this mystery will tell you what they saw. Their clues will help your class solve the mystery.

How Much Ocean, How Much Land?

If you were looking at the earth from space, it would look like a big blue marble. The pictures show the earth as it looks from space. What do the colors tell you about the earth's surface? How much of the earth do you think is covered by land? by water?

Exploration:
Compare land and water.

You need:
Globe

❶ Elect a record-keeper to enter the results of this Exploration on a tally sheet. The tally sheet should have two columns, headed "Land" and "Water."

❷ Each class member takes a turn. When it's your turn, close your eyes, hold the globe, and spin it several times. Touch one point on the globe. The record-keeper marks either the "Land" column or the "Water" column.

❸ Repeat step 2 two more times, so that you've chosen a total of three points on the globe.

❹ Add up the marks in each column of the tally sheet.

Interpret your results.

• If there were equal amounts of water and land on the earth, how would you expect the number of marks in each column to compare?

• If there were more water than land, how would you expect the number of marks to compare?

• How can you use the tally sheet to compare the amounts of water and land? About how much of the earth's surface is water? How much is land?

• How accurate do you think your estimates are? Do you think the accuracy would change if step 2 were repeated ten times instead of three?

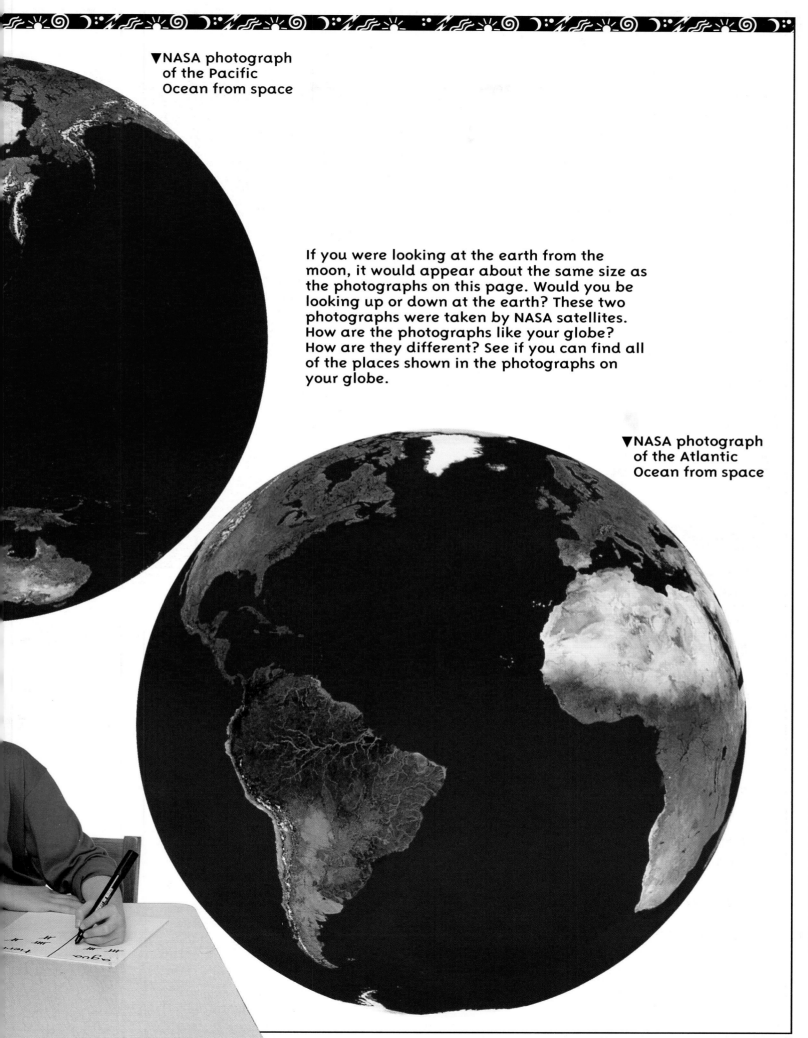

▼NASA photograph of the Pacific Ocean from space

If you were looking at the earth from the moon, it would appear about the same size as the photographs on this page. Would you be looking up or down at the earth? These two photographs were taken by NASA satellites. How are the photographs like your globe? How are they different? See if you can find all of the places shown in the photographs on your globe.

▼NASA photograph of the Atlantic Ocean from space

Exploration Connection:
Interpreting maps

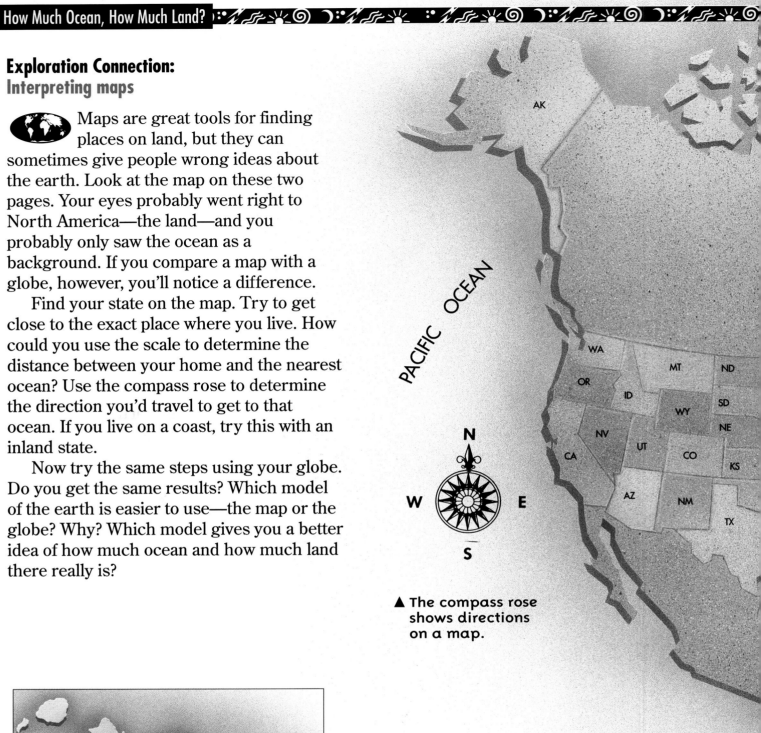

Maps are great tools for finding places on land, but they can sometimes give people wrong ideas about the earth. Look at the map on these two pages. Your eyes probably went right to North America—the land—and you probably only saw the ocean as a background. If you compare a map with a globe, however, you'll notice a difference.

Find your state on the map. Try to get close to the exact place where you live. How could you use the scale to determine the distance between your home and the nearest ocean? Use the compass rose to determine the direction you'd travel to get to that ocean. If you live on a coast, try this with an inland state.

Now try the same steps using your globe. Do you get the same results? Which model of the earth is easier to use—the map or the globe? Why? Which model gives you a better idea of how much ocean and how much land there really is?

▲ The compass rose shows directions on a map.

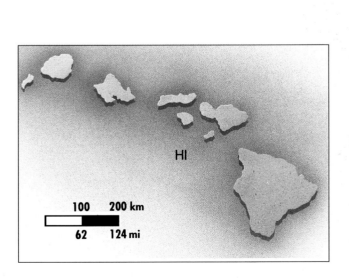

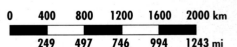

0	400	800	1200	1600	2000 km
	249	497	746	994	1243 mi

▲The scale shows how to tell distances on the map. This scale tells you that 1 centimeter represents 400 kilometers (249 miles) on this map. If you measure 3 centimeters between two places on this map, what is the actual distance between the places?

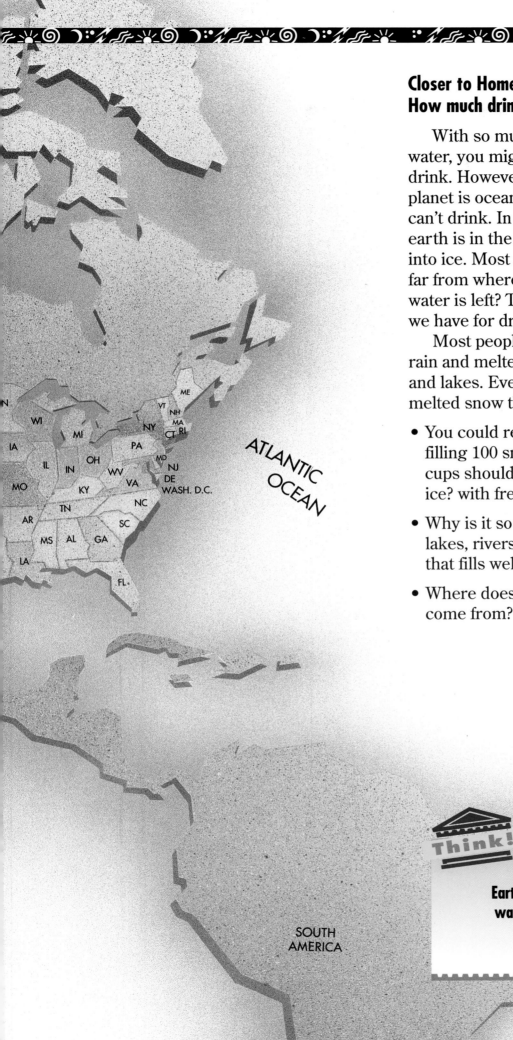

ATLANTIC
OCEAN

SOUTH
AMERICA

Closer to Home:
How much drinking water?

With so much of the earth covered with water, you might think there'd be plenty to drink. However, most of the water on your planet is ocean water—salty water that you can't drink. In fact, 97/100 of the water on the earth is in the ocean. Another 2/100 is frozen into ice. Most of the ice is at the South Pole, far from where most people live. How much water is left? That's the amount of water that we have for drinking.

Most people get their drinking water from rain and melted snow that collects in rivers and lakes. Even well water started as rain or melted snow that soaked into the ground.

- You could represent the earth's water by filling 100 small cups with water. How many cups should be filled with salt water? with ice? with fresh water?

- Why is it so important for people to protect lakes, rivers, and the underground water that fills wells?

- Where does the drinking water in your area come from? How could you find out?

Think!

Earth is sometimes known as "the water planet." Why do you think this is so?

Why Is the Ocean Salty?

The water that you drink is fresh water. Its <u>salinity</u>— the amount of salt it contains—is very low. You know that your community's supply of fresh water starts as rain or snow. Rain and snow contain almost no salt. However, lakes and rivers fed by rain and snow contain small amounts of salt, and the ocean is very salty. How do you think salt gets into rivers, lakes, and the ocean?

Rain and Snow

Exploration:
Make a rain model.

You need:
Paint tray
Sand
Cup
Water
Tape or labels
2 spoons
2 small dishes
Hand lens

❶ Make a model of land and ocean. Start by putting sand in the shallow end of your tray. Leave the deep end empty—it will represent the ocean.

❷ Slowly pour at least 10 cups of water onto the sand. Wait 10 minutes. How has your model changed? ✐

❸ Label the two dishes as shown in the picture. Put a spoonful of fresh water in the correct dish and a spoonful of water from your model in the empty dish. Put both dishes in a warm place until all the water evaporates. Then use a hand lens to observe anything left in the dishes. ✐

Interpret your results.

- Which dish had more dry matter in it after the water evaporated? Where did this dry matter come from?

- How does some salt enter the ocean?

- How many different ways do rivers change the ocean?

water from model

fresh water

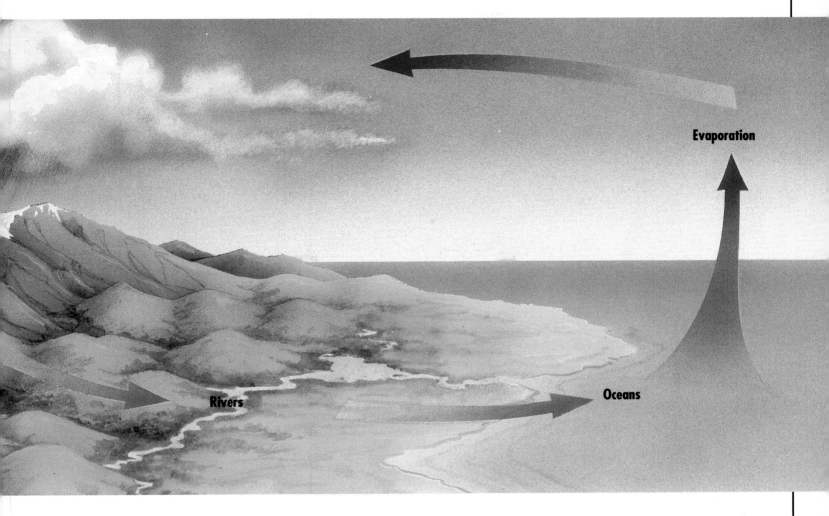

Evaporation

Oceans

Rivers

Exploration Connection:
Using reference books

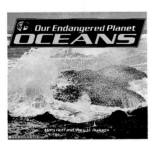

Your model shows how rain affects the ocean. The ocean also affects rain. You might live hundreds of kilometers inland, but the rain that falls on you was probably water that evaporated from the ocean. Wind can carry evaporated water all the way across a continent. How do lakes and forests affect the water cycle? You can find out on pages 15–17 of *Oceans*.

Study the diagram of the water cycle. Which parts of the water cycle did your model show? You could make your model show the whole water cycle by covering it with clear plastic food wrap. **Try it!**

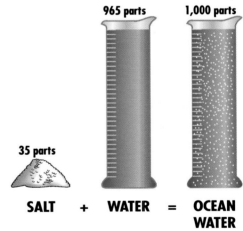

965 parts   1,000 parts

35 parts

SALT + WATER = OCEAN WATER

Salinity is measured in parts per thousand. The picture shows that for every 1,000 parts of ocean water, 35 parts are salt and other minerals, and 965 parts are water. If you filled a tank with ocean water weighing 1,000 kilograms and allowed the water to evaporate, how much salt would be left at the bottom of the tank?

Now you know one way salt gets into the ocean. Scientists have considered many other processes that may have made the ocean salty. Here's one possibility.

Exploration:
Model a sea floor.

You need:

2 clear plastic containers
Plastic wrap
Rocks
Fresh water
2 spoons
2 small dishes
Hand lens

❶ Place three or four rocks in one of the containers. Cover them with fresh water. Label the container and cover it with plastic wrap.

❷ Put fresh water in the other container. Label the container and cover it with plastic wrap. Put both containers in a sunny window or another warm spot. Wait an hour.

❸ Study both containers. What do you observe?

❹ Label the dishes as shown. Put a spoonful of water from one container in one dish. Put a spoonful of water from the other container in the other dish.

❺ Put both dishes in a warm place until all the water evaporates. Then use a hand lens to observe anything left in the dishes.

Interpret your results.

- How did the water affect the rocks?

- Which dish had more dry matter in it after the water evaporated? Where did this dry matter come from?

- Many parts of the ocean floor are rocky. What do some of these rocks contain? How do you think ocean water affects these rocks?

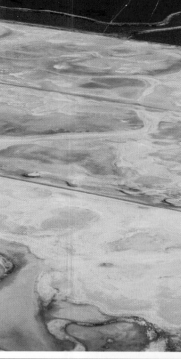

Closer to Home: Eating the ocean

When you go home today, take a look at the salt and pepper shakers. One of them contains a small bit of the ocean. Companies that sell table salt get the salt from two places: from ocean water or from salt left behind by ancient oceans that evaporated.

Most of the salt that people use on food comes from ocean water. The pictures show how salt is taken out of ocean water. The rest of the salt that people use comes from salt mines. Millions of years ago parts of the ocean evaporated, leaving behind thick layers of salt. Over time these salt layers were covered by layers of rock. In order to get to the salt people have to dig mines through the layers of rock. These mines can be small mines where a few people work, or they can be huge, with thousands of workers.

- What happens to the water that evaporates from the salt ponds?

- Which do you think is harder—getting salt from ocean water or getting salt from a mine?

◀ **Top:**
To get large amounts of sea salt, workers flood wide shallow ponds with ocean water.

Middle:
The water evaporates, leaving salt on the bottom of each pond.

Bottom:
Truckloads of salt are collected. The trucks carry the salt to factories where it is cleaned and packaged.

Think!

The ocean is much saltier than most rivers and lakes. Why?

How Does Salt Affect Ocean Water?

The amount of salt in ocean water makes ocean water very different from the water found in rivers and lakes. For example, how do you think ocean water would taste compared to fresh water? How else do you think the salt in ocean water makes it different from fresh water?

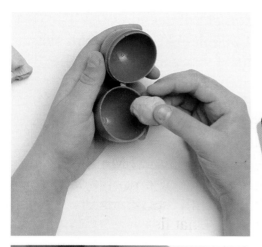

Exploration:
Compare salt water and fresh water.

You need:

1 liter of water
Clear plastic container
Clay
Plastic egg
Salt
Spoon

❶ Pour 1 liter of fresh water into the container. Put just enough clay in the egg to make it sink to the bottom of the container. You'll need to try adding and taking away small pieces of clay to get the right amount.

❷ Take the egg out of the container. Add six spoonfuls of salt to the water. Stir until the salt disappears. The water is now as salty as ocean water.

❸ Put the egg with the clay inside back into the water. What happens? ✏️

Interpret your results.

- When the salt seemed to disappear, what really happened to it?

- Do objects float more easily in salt water or in fresh water? How do you know?

- What would you have to do to the egg to change what happened in step 3? **Try it!**

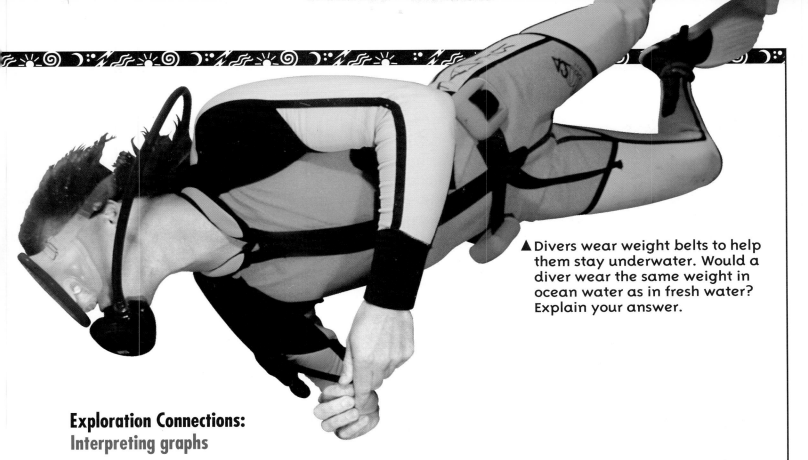

▲ Divers wear weight belts to help them stay underwater. Would a diver wear the same weight in ocean water as in fresh water? Explain your answer.

Exploration Connections:
Interpreting graphs

The Gulf of Mexico is a very large ocean basin that is almost completely enclosed by the United States and Mexico. The coastline along the Gulf is nearly 5,000 kilometers (3,100 miles) long. Many rivers—from both the United States and Mexico—flow into the Gulf.

The bar graph shows the amount of salt in the Gulf of Mexico and in some of the rivers that enter the Gulf of Mexico. Each place on the graph is also shown on the table. The table also lists fish that are found in those places. What fish live in the rivers? in the Gulf? Why don't the Gulf fish live in the rivers? Why don't the river fish live in the Gulf? Can you figure out this mystery by comparing the graph and the table?

FISH IN THE GULF OF MEXICO AND SOME RIVERS

Fish	Mississippi River	Mermentau River	Suwannee River	Gulf of Mexico
Catfish	●	●		
Walleyes	●	●		
Suckers	●	●		
Carp	●	●	●	
Garfish	●	●		
Bass			●	
Pike			●	
Trout		●		
Nassau Grouper				●
Marlin				●
Sea Bass				●
Sharks				●
Sea Trout				●

SALINITY OF THE GULF OF MEXICO AND SOME RIVERS

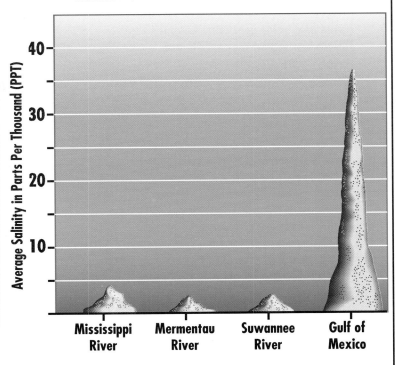

Closer to Home:
Why can't people drink salt water?

Salt makes ocean water undrinkable for humans. If you were stuck on an island with no fresh water, you couldn't quench your thirst by drinking ocean water. The more ocean water you drank, the thirstier you'd feel.

SALT WATER AND YOUR CELLS

KEY
Salt = ☐
Water = ●

Your body is made of cells. Inside each cell is fluid that's mostly water. Outside each cell is fluid that's mostly water. Both fluids contain the same amount of salt.

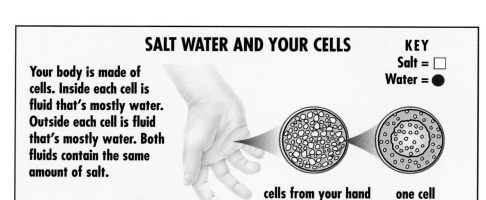

cells from your hand   one cell

If you drink ocean water, the salt passes from your intestines into your blood. Now the fluid outside your cells is saltier than the fluid inside.

The cell has less salt than the fluid around it.

Salt attracts water. The extra salt outside your cells pulls water out of the fluid inside your cells. As your cells lose water, they shrink, and can't work properly.

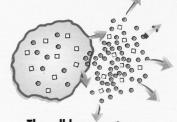

The cell loses water.

As the water leaves your cells, salt stays in the cells. Now there's too much salt inside your cells, so your cells pump out salt—and they shrink even more. If you keep drinking ocean water, your cells will shrink until they die.

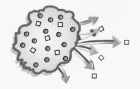

The cell loses salt.

◄ If you look closely at the mangrove leaf, you'll notice a crust of salt on it.

▼ Mangrove trees growing in the Gulf of Mexico

You can watch salt affect cells that aren't designed to live in the ocean. If you sprinkle salt on a small piece of raw beef, you'll see the meat begin to change within a few minutes. **Try it!**

Anything that lives in the ocean must have cells that aren't hurt by the salt in ocean water, or body parts that get rid of the extra salt. The plants in the pictures are mangrove trees growing in shallow ocean water. Mangrove trees can grow in ocean water or in salty sand because their leaves have special cells that get rid of extra salt.

• Could you do anything to ocean water to make it drinkable? Explain your answer.

Think!

Some fish can live in both salt water and fresh water. Why is this unusual?

How Does Ocean Water Move?

River water that enters the ocean can travel halfway around the world in just a few weeks. How do you think that happens? In 1991, hundreds of sneakers washed up on Pacific beaches. They had been in the cargo of a ship that sank far out at sea the year before. How did the shoes get from the middle of the ocean to the shore?

Exploration:
Make a storm winds model.

You need:

Index card
Scissors
Tape
Paint tray
Water

❶ Cut a small square from one corner of the index card. Roll the rest of the index card into a tube and fasten it with tape.

❷ Fill the tray with water. When the water is completely still, float the square near the middle of the tray.

❸ Hold the tube close to the water near one end of the tray. Blow very gently straight down on the water—but not on the square—for 3 or 4 seconds.

❹ Observe what happens to the water and to the floating square. Record your observations. ✐

Interpret your results.

• What happened to the top of the water when you blew on it? What happened to the floating square?

• What do you think is one cause of ocean <u>waves</u>?

• Waves are always forming somewhere in the ocean. Why?

• How do waves affect objects floating in the ocean?

Exploration Connection:
Using reference books

Waves aren't the only kind of motion in the ocean. Compare the two pictures at left. They both show the same place. And they were both taken on the same day.

How do you think the owners of the boats will get the boats back in the water? To find out what causes the change shown in the pictures—and how often it happens—read "Ups and Downs" on pages 18–19 of *Oceans*. Then record what you find on your ThinkMat table. How do you think these ups and downs could be seen at a beach?

◄ These pictures show a harbor at two different times on the same day. What happened?

So far, you've discovered two ways the ocean moves every day. There's a third way that happens in many parts of the ocean. Remember those shoes? Waves put them on the beach, but a <u>current</u> carried them away from the wreck of the ship. What do you think a current is?

Exploration:
Make a prevailing winds model.

You need:

Paint tray
Water
Pepper
Spoon
1 straw per person in
your group

❶ Fill the tray almost to the top with water. When the water is completely still, drop a spoonful of pepper onto the water.

❷ What do you think will happen to the pepper if you and your partners take turns blowing across the same place in the water? Record your prediction. ✎

❸ Hold the straw in one place above the water. Blow lightly across the water for 10 seconds. A partner should have his or her straw ready to start blowing on the same place before you run out of air.

❹ Repeat step 3 five or six times. Your team should keep a constant flow of air blowing on the same place in the water. Observe what happens to the water and the pepper. Record your observations. ✎

Interpret your results.

• Was your prediction correct? If not, what happened that you didn't expect?

• By blowing constantly on the water in your model, you made a current. How would you describe a current?

• Did the current move only in the direction you blew?

• How do you think most currents form in the ocean?

North
Pacific

California

Pacific North
Equatorial

Pacific South Equatorial

South Pacific

West Wind Drift

Closer to Home:
Wind, currents, and rain

Ocean currents are part of the water cycle. Even if you live in the middle of North America, some of the rain that falls on you came from ocean currents.

The map shows some of the main ocean currents. The winds that push these currents also pick up water as it evaporates. As the wind pushes a current through the ocean, the wind picks up and carries more and more evaporated water.

When a current reaches a shore, the land blocks the water and the current has to turn. The same thing happened in your current model: When your current hit the side of the pan, the water turned. The arrows on the map show this.

Find the North Pacific current. When it reaches North America, it turns south and becomes the California current. However, the wind with its load of evaporated water doesn't turn. Instead, it blows right over the land. When the warm, wet wind meets colder air, the evaporated water forms clouds and rain. Rain from the Pacific Ocean can fall in the middle of North America.

- Study the map. Which current carries storms from the Atlantic to North America?

Think!

How is the way currents form the same as the way waves form? How is it different?

OCEAN CURRENTS

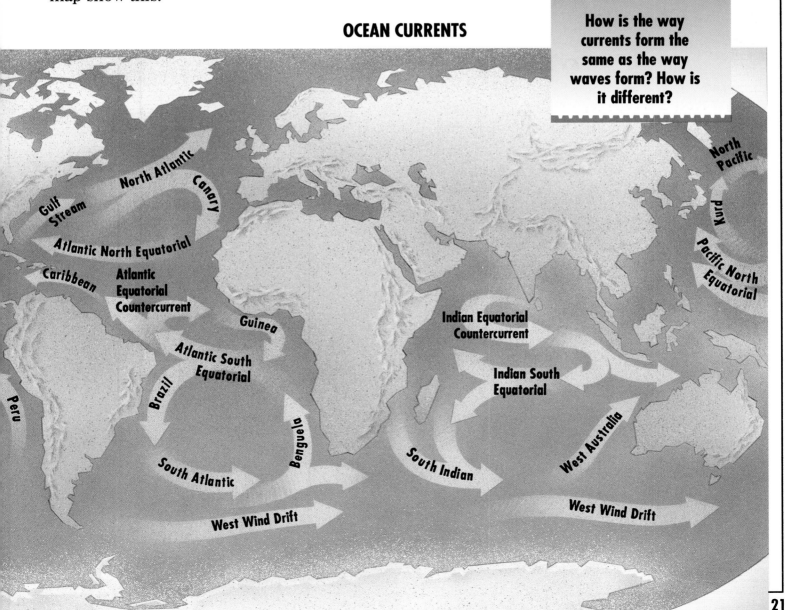

How Does Ocean Water Change With Depth?

The currents you've learned about are called surface currents. That means they happen at the top of the ocean. Waves also happen on the surface. Learning about the ocean far below the surface is much harder than learning about the surface. What kinds of problems do you think are faced by people who want to study the deeper parts of the ocean?

Exploration:
Test the depths.

You need:
Large container
Water
Rubber glove

❶ Pour water into the container until it is almost full.

❷ Put on the rubber glove and pull it so that it covers your wrist.

❸ Stick your gloved hand into the container until your hand and wrist are underwater. What happens to the glove? How does your hand feel? ✏

▲ The nautilus lives deep below the surface in certain parts of the Pacific Ocean. Its shell helps protect it from pressure. It rises by pumping its chambers full of gases, which are not as heavy as water, and it sinks by pumping gases out of its chambers.

Interpret your results.

• <u>Pressure</u> caused the glove to do what it did. How would you describe pressure?

• What do you think would happen if you put your gloved hand into a deeper container of water? **Try it!**

Exploration Connection:
Interpreting tables

You're under pressure right now. Every square inch of your body is being pressed by about 7 kg (15 pounds) of air. This is a pressure of 1 atmosphere. Look at the table below. How much pressure would be pushing on an object 2,400 meters below the surface?

Take another look at the table. How else does ocean water change as you go deeper? How do you think this change would affect people trying to explore the ocean? You know what plants need to live. Would you expect to find any plants living at the surface? 300 meters down? 1,500 meters down?

OCEAN DEPTH AND PRESSURE

Depth Below Surface (meters)		Pressure (atmospheres)
Surface		1
	Scuba Diver (55 meters)	
300		31
600		61
900	Submarines	91
1200		121
1500		151
1800		181
2100		211
2400		241
2700		271
3000	Deep sea diving vessels can reach the ocean floor.	301
3300		331
3600	Average Depth of Ocean	361

If you were to scuba dive more than 55 meters (180 feet) below the surface, pressure would squeeze you so hard you couldn't breathe. If you swim too deep, the pressure would crush your bones. If you wanted to go below 460 meters (1,500 feet), you'd have to use a submersible like the one in the picture. You can make a device that shows how depth and water pressure are related.

▲ *Alvin* can dive below 3,300 meters (11,000 feet).

Exploration:
Observe water pressure.

You need:

Milk carton with top cut off
Pencils
Water

❶ Use a pencil to make a hole in one side of a milk carton. Leave the pencil in the carton to plug the hole. Fill the carton with water.

❷ Pull the pencil out of the carton and observe the water.

❸ If you wanted the water to shoot out farther, where in the carton would you make another hole? **Try it!** Record what you observe. ✎

Interpret your results.

- Pressure forced the water out of the holes. Where in your milk carton was the pressure greater? How do you know?

- If you wanted water to shoot out even farther, where in the carton would you make a third hole? **Try it!**

- How does depth affect pressure?

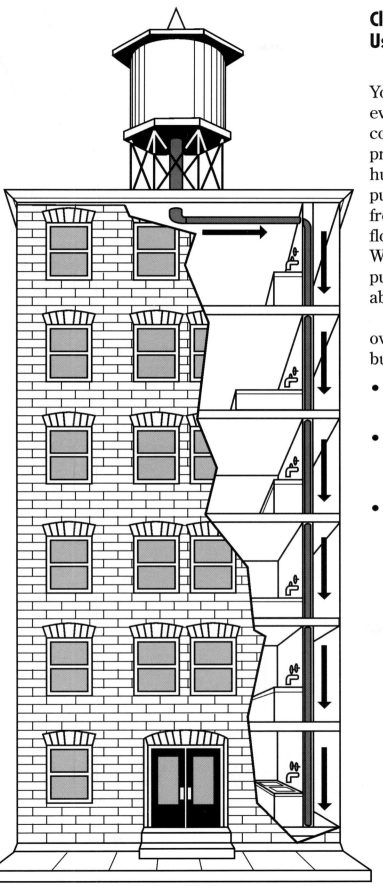

Closer to Home: Using water pressure

People use water pressure to do work. You can see the effects of water pressure every time you turn on a faucet. Water coming out of a faucet is pushed by pressure. Many towns have tall towers with huge water tanks at the top. Water is pumped up into the tanks. Pipes lead down from the tanks to faucets in buildings. Water flows down from the tank to the faucets. When you turn on a faucet, the water is pushed out by the pressure of all the water above and behind it.

In large cities, many buildings have their own water tanks. The diagram shows how a building's water tank works.

- Why does a water tank have to be higher than the faucets?

- Look at the diagram. Where is water pressure greater—on the top floor or on the bottom floor?

- What makes the water pressure in your school—a city supply or a tank on top of the school?

▲ Cutaway of building showing water system

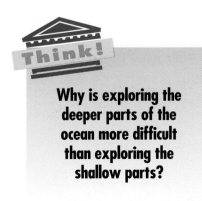

Think!

Why is exploring the deeper parts of the ocean more difficult than exploring the shallow parts?

How Does the Ocean's Depth Vary?

There are very few parts of the ocean floor that people have ever been to. However, people have learned how deep most parts of the ocean floor are. They also know some of the ways the ocean floor has changed. How do you think people got this information?

Exploration:
Explore the floor.

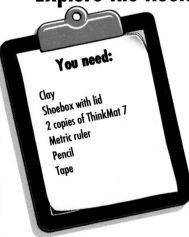

You need:

Clay
Shoebox with lid
2 copies of ThinkMat 7
Metric ruler
Pencil
Tape

❶ Choose a small section of the ocean floor shown in the large picture. Use clay to build a model of that section in your box.

❷ Put the lid on the box. Tape one copy of ThinkMat 7 to the lid. Tape the lid closed.

❸ Trade boxes with another team. How can your team use the two ThinkMats, the pencil, and the ruler to find out the depths of the other team's ocean floor model? You can't take the lid off the box, but you can make small holes in the lid.

❹ After you've figured out the depths, you can use that information to draw a picture of the model without taking off the lid. How could you do this?

Interpret your results.

• Were you able to figure out the depths of most parts of the ocean floor model? How?

• People don't use rulers to figure out how deep the real ocean floor is. What do you think they use instead?

▶ These pictures show some of the main features of the ocean floor. Look closely at the bottom picture. Can you see a kind of pattern?

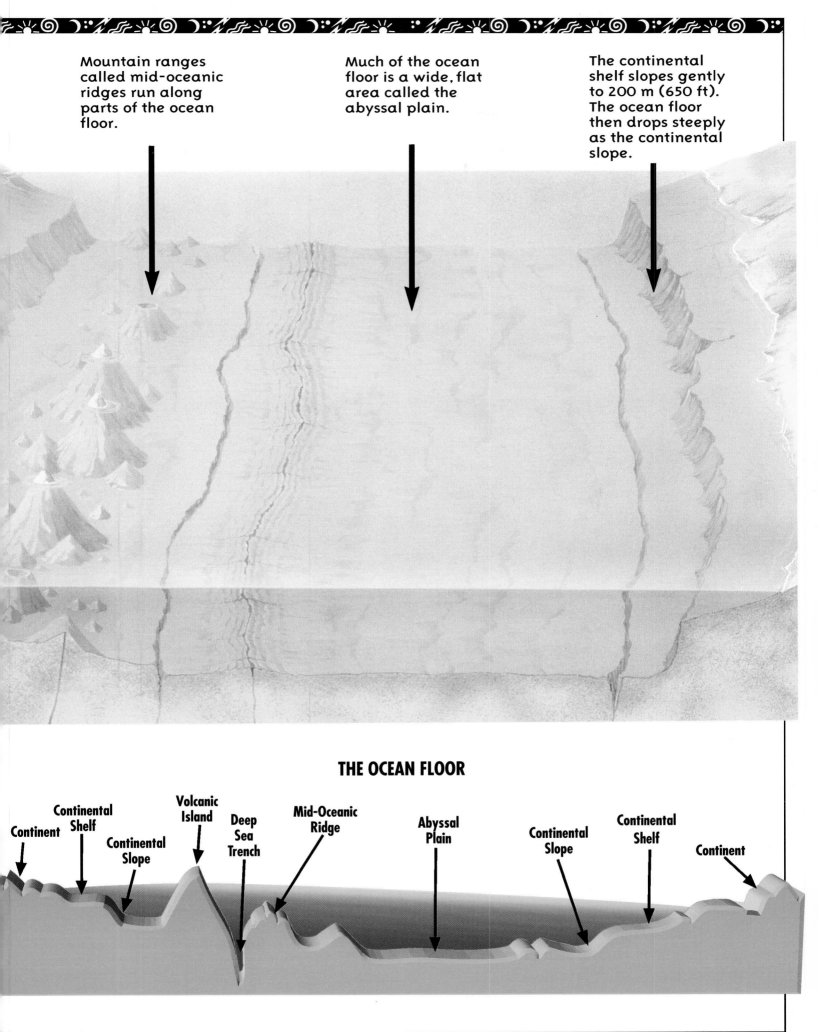

Mountain ranges called mid-oceanic ridges run along parts of the ocean floor.

Much of the ocean floor is a wide, flat area called the abyssal plain.

The continental shelf slopes gently to 200 m (650 ft). The ocean floor then drops steeply as the continental slope.

THE OCEAN FLOOR

Continent

Continental Shelf

Continental Slope

Volcanic Island

Deep Sea Trench

Mid-Oceanic Ridge

Abyssal Plain

Continental Slope

Continental Shelf

Continent

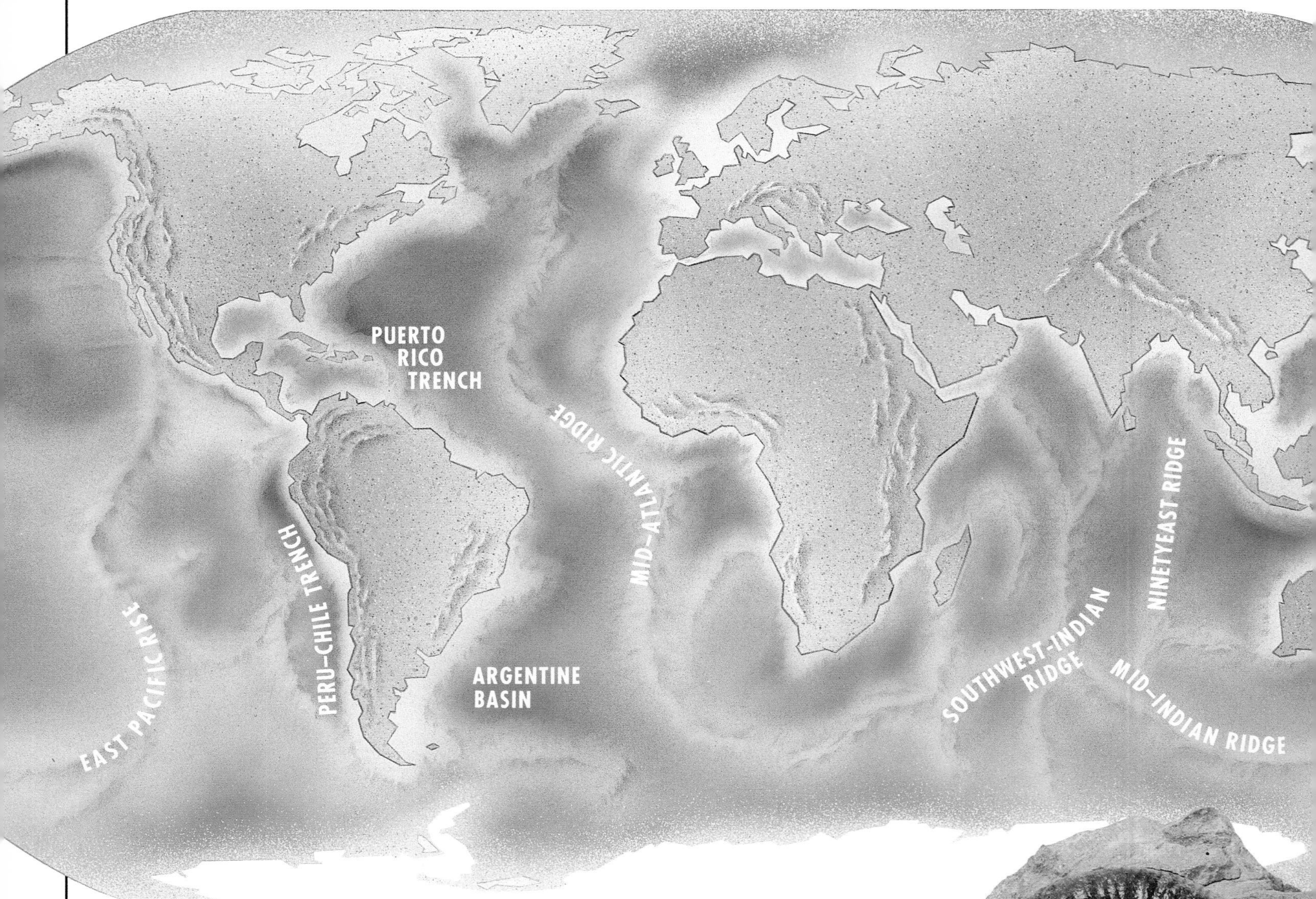

PUERTO
RICO
TRENCH

MID-ATLANTIC RIDGE

NINETYEAST RIDGE

PERU–CHILE TRENCH

SOUTHWEST–INDIAN
RIDGE

MID–INDIAN RIDGE

EAST PACIFIC RISE

ARGENTINE
BASIN

RELIEF MAP OF THE EARTH

Exploration Connection:
Interpreting maps

A relief map shows the shape of the earth's surface. This relief map shows the ocean floor and the continents. What kinds of landforms are found on both the ocean floor and the continents? What landforms started on the ocean floor but are now above the ocean's surface?

People use <u>sonar</u> to make relief maps of underwater landforms. Sound waves are bounced off the ocean floor. The deeper the water, the more time it takes the sound to return to the surface. A computer uses all the sonar times to make a picture of the different depths of the ocean floor. How is using sonar like what you did on page 26?

▲ Ammonites lived on continental shelves throughout the world.

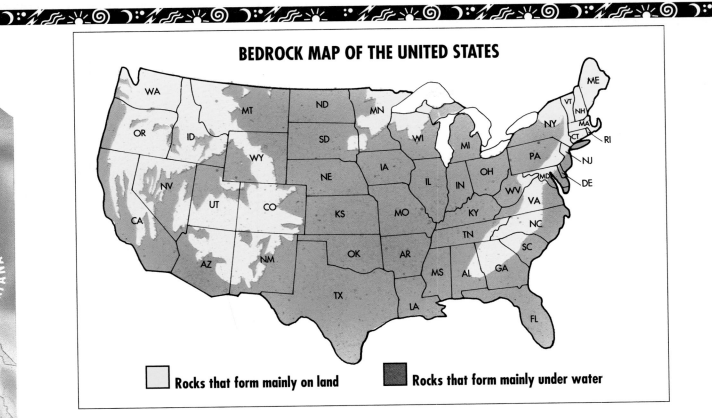

BEDROCK MAP OF THE UNITED STATES

☐ **Rocks that form mainly on land**   ■ **Rocks that form mainly under water**

Closer to Home:
How deep do you live?

It isn't now, but the area where you live might once have been part of the ocean floor. Sonar helps people understand how deep the ocean floor is now. By studying an area's bedrock—the rock under the soil—people can learn how that place has changed. Bedrock in many parts of the United States contains fossils like the ones shown here. These fossils come from animals that lived over a continental shelf.

The small map shows where two different kinds of bedrock are found. One kind forms mostly under water and often contains fossils like the ones on this page. The other kind forms mostly on land.

- What do these fossils show about the areas where they were found?

- Study the map. What kind of rock is in your area? What does this tell you about the history of your area?

◄ In this relief map, the continental shelf is the light blue area around each continent. What do the other colors show?

▼ This trilobite lived on the ocean floor near the edge of a continental shelf. Its fossil was found in Utah.

Think!

Has the ocean's depth stopped changing? Explain your answer.

What Is the Continental Shelf?

If you find the fossil of a sea animal, the animal probably once lived on or above the <u>continental shelf</u>. Even today, that's where most of the living things in the ocean make their home. Why do you think that's true? Every part of the continental shelf has living things crawling on it, or swimming or floating above it. Finding out what the shelf is like will help you understand why so many things live there.

Exploration:
Identify continental shelf conditions.

❶ Find the continental shelf on the diagram below. Is it shallower or deeper than the rest of the ocean? ✎

❷ The depth of water affects light. How important do you think light is to life on the continental shelf?

❸ What do you know about depth and water pressure? What do you think water pressure is like on the continental shelf?

❹ Look again at the map on pages 28–29. How large a part of the ocean floor is the continental shelf?

❺ Shores are parts of the continental shelf. Look at the shores on the next page. How much do waves affect the continental shelf? How about tides? currents?

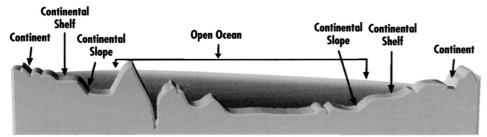

Continent · Continental Shelf · Continental Slope · Open Ocean · Continental Slope · Continental Shelf · Continent

Grouper

Trumpetfish

Turtle Grass

Sea Anemones

Sand Star

Interpret your results.

• Do you think there are a lot of plants on the continental shelf, or only a few?

• How do you think the number of plants affects the number of animals?

• Many animals with hard shells live near the shore on the continental shelf, especially near the shore. How do their shells help them survive?

▶ There are many kinds of shores on the continental shelf. How do you think animals that live on a sandy shore are different from those that live on a rocky shore?

CONTINENTAL SHELF, WARM WATER ENVIRONMENT

Barracuda

Jellyfish

Lemon Shark

Blue Shark

Herring

Butterflyfish

Golden Boxfish

Threespot Damselfish

Bluestriped Grunt

Rainbow Parrotfish

Octopus

Ghost Crab

Tulip Snail

Moray Eel

Hermit Crab

Exploration Connection:
Using reference books

What's the biggest thing ever built? If you guessed a skyscraper or even a city, you're thinking big—but not big enough. On the continental shelf off the coast of Australia is the Great Barrier Reef. It's over 2,000 kilometers (1,250 miles) long. It's been there for thousands of years and the workers—tiny animals called <u>corals</u>—are still building it.

The Great Barrier Reef is a <u>coral reef</u>. It looks like it's made of stone, but it's not. Coral reefs are made of the stony skeletons of millions of coral animals. A coral animal is shaped like a tube. Tiny tentacles surround its mouth. They grab and sting even tinier creatures that drift by in the current.

When corals die, their skeletons remain. New corals build their skeletons on top of the old ones. Over thousands of years, these layers build up into beautiful coral reefs.

There are many kinds of corals in a reef. Some of the shapes that are made by coral skeletons look like giant brains. Others look like antlers, fingers, or flowers. Thousands of animals live in and around coral reefs. You can learn about some of these strange and beautiful animals on pages 5–7, 14–17, and 21–22 of *Under the Sea from A to Z.*

▲ How many kinds of living things can you find in this small piece of Australia's Great Barrier Reef?

◀ Each flowerlike structure is the ring of tentacles around a coral animal's mouth.

Closer to Home:
Collecting the ocean

Have you ever seen seashells or coral for sale? If so, you've seen things that used to live on the continental shelf.

Corals that are sold in stores are collected alive. That's so they'll be in good shape when they reach the stores. The corals are broken off the reef and soaked in bleach to kill the coral animals and anything else that makes the coral its home.

Most mollusks—animals that build seashells—are also collected alive. The animals die and their bodies are taken out of the shells. Some kinds of mollusks have become rare because so many of them have

been sold for their shells. And some of these mollusks eat starfish, which kill corals. So, in places where all of these mollusks have been caught, the reefs are beginning to die.

- How does breaking a piece of coral off a reef affect other things that live on the reef?

- How do you think collecting shells affects the continental shelf?

Why is the continental shelf so crowded with life?

How Is the Open Ocean Different From the Continental Shelf?

On the continental shelf, every bit of space is home to something. Imagine that you're in a boat above the continental shelf. You're floating away from shore. Soon you're above the continental slope, and then you're moving into the <u>open</u> <u>ocean</u>. There could be as much as 12 kilometers (7 1/2 miles) of water between you and the ocean floor. What do you think the open ocean is like?

Exploration:
Identify open ocean conditions.

❶ Find the open ocean on the diagram below. Compared to the water above the continental shelf, is the open ocean deeper or shallower?

❷ Do you think light is important in any part of the open ocean? If so, what part?

❸ How does water pressure affect the open ocean?

❹ Look at the diagram below. Is the open ocean larger or smaller than the rest of the ocean?

❺ Do waves greatly affect any part of the open ocean? Do tides? Do currents? Explain your answers.

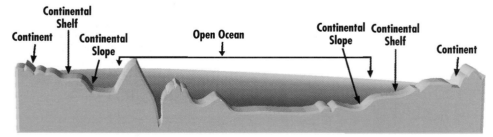

Interpret your results.

• Where in the open ocean would you expect to find plants or other organisms that need sunlight?

• Where in the open ocean do you think you'd find most animals ? Explain.

• Many animals live on the continental shelf. Would you expect to find as many animals living on the floor of the open ocean? Why or why not?

By-the-wind sailor

Ocean sunfish

▲ The largest animals on the earth—whales—live in the open ocean. Why is the open ocean a good environment for very large animals?

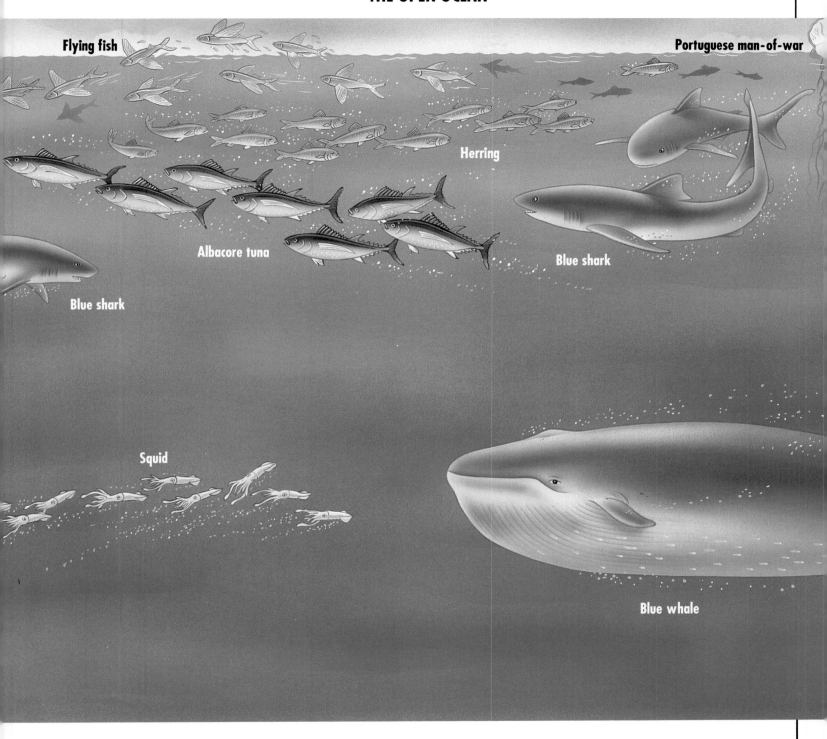

Flying fish

Portuguese man-of-war

Herring

Blue shark

Albacore tuna

Blue shark

Squid

Blue whale

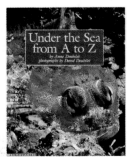

Exploration Connection:
Using reference books

Fish aren't the only animals in the open ocean. Marine mammals such as dolphins and whales live there, too. Seals are often found in the open ocean.

The biggest fish of all also lives there. Any idea what it is? To find out more about these open ocean animals, turn to pages 4, 19, and 23 of *Under the Sea from A to Z*.

To survive in the open ocean, fish and other swimming animals have to have a certain kind of body shape. What kind of shape do you think they need?

Exploration:
Compare aquatic body shapes.

You need:

Paint tray
Newspaper
Water
Flat-bottomed cup
Cone-shaped cup
Thread
Tape

❶ Put the paint tray on a few sheets of newspaper to catch any spills. Fill the paint tray with water.

❷ Cut two lengths of thread at least 50 centimeters long. Use tape to attach an end of each length to the center of the bottom of each cup.

❸ Drag the flat-bottomed cup through the water, using the thread. How does the cup move? ✏

❹ Drag the cone-shaped cup through the water, using the thread. How does the cup move? ✏

Interpret your results.

• Which shape moved through the water faster?

• All the animals on this page live in the open ocean. How are they alike?

• How does speed help an animal survive?

▲ Whale shark

▲ Marlin

Closer to Home:
Marine parks

More than 500 dolphins and whales live in marine parks and aquariums in the United States. At most parks and aquariums, the animals perform tricks. To do many of the tricks, the animals use <u>echolocation</u>. Echolocation is much like sonar: An animal makes sounds that bounce off objects in the water. The animal can tell from the echo where and what the objects are.

Some people think that keeping whales and dolphins in captivity is cruel. They also think that it isn't right to make the animals do tricks. Other people say that the animals are treated with respect, get plenty to eat, and are protected from natural enemies.

Scientists have discovered a lot about marine mammals from observing them in aquariums and marine parks. Visitors to these places also learn about the intelligence of marine mammals, how they live in families, and how they talk to each other.

- Is learning about ocean animals a good reason to keep them captive? Explain your answer.

▲ Dolphin performing at marine park

- After visiting a marine park or aquarium, many people decide to help protect the ocean and its animals. Is this a good reason to keep some animals captive?

- Do you think marine animals have as good a life in captivity as they would in the ocean?

▲ Mackerel

Think!

Why is the open ocean a good environment for the blue whale?

What Is the Abyss Like?

The waters of the continental shelf are the most crowded parts of the ocean. The open ocean is much less crowded. The <u>abyss</u>— any part of the ocean that is deeper than 2 kilometers (1 1/2 miles)—is the least crowded of all. Find the abyss in the diagram below. What do you think the abyss environment is like?

▲ Johnson's black anglerfish

Exploration:

Identify conditions in the abyss.

❶ Compared to the waters of the continental shelf and the open ocean, is the abyss deeper or shallower? Record your answer on the table on your LabMat.

❷ How important is light in the abyss?

❸ How much do you think pressure affects life in the abyss?

❹ Look at the diagram below. Is the abyss larger or smaller than the continental shelf? Is it larger or smaller than the open ocean?

❺ Do you think waves greatly affect the abyss? Do tides? Do currents? Explain your answers.

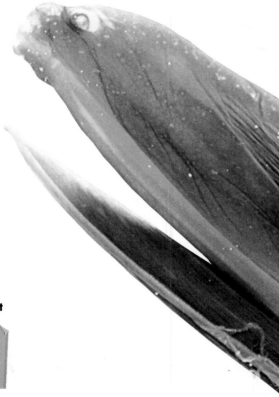

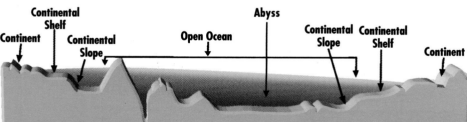

Continent | Continental Shelf | Continental Slope | Open Ocean | Abyss | Continental Slope | Continental Shelf | Continent

Interpret your results.

- Do plants or other organisms that need sunlight live in the abyss? Explain your answer using the data on your table.

- Do you think the abyss is warm, cool, or very cold? Explain.

- Why is there less life in the abyss than there is in the rest of the ocean?

Megamouth shark ▶

Exploration Connection:
Interpreting photographs

The photographs on these two pages are rare. Why would photographing animals in the abyss be hard to do? The ocean is full of strange-looking animals, but as you can see, the strangest of all live in the abyss.

Finding food in the abyss is a big problem. Abyss fishes often wait a long time between meals, so they have to be able to eat just about anything—big or small. Compare the pictures. What body parts help some of these animals catch and eat fish that are as big as they are?

Like the viper fish, many of the animals in the abyss can produce light. How does that help them survive in the abyss? You've figured out what pressure is like in the abyss. Some of these fish have soft, flexible skeletons. Why would a soft skeleton be better under pressure than a hard skeleton?

▲ Viper fish chasing hatchet fish

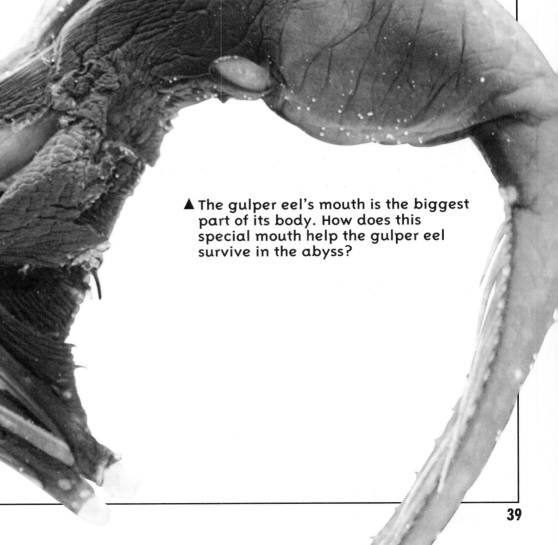
▲ The gulper eel's mouth is the biggest part of its body. How does this special mouth help the gulper eel survive in the abyss?

◀ *Alvin* exploring the wreck of the *Titanic*

Closer to Home:
Sunken treasure

Have you ever dreamed of finding sunken treasure? For years people dreamed of finding the *Titanic*, a ship that struck an iceberg in 1912 and sank into the abyss. But how do you find something in the abyss? Even such a huge ship is only a speck on the ocean floor.

In 1985, a team of scientists led by Robert Ballard started searching for the *Titanic*. Ballard felt that the sinking ship must have left a long trail of waste, and that's what he looked for. His team used a robot search vehicle called *Argo,* which they lowered into the abyss and dragged over a huge area. They finally found the wrecked ship nearly 4,000 meters (12,500 feet) below the surface.

A year later, Dr. Ballard visited the wreck in *Alvin,* a tiny three-person submarine. A robot attached to *Alvin* was used to explore the *Titanic*. The drawings show *Alvin* exploring the *Titanic*. Why aren't there photographs of this event?

- Why did Dr. Ballard look for the waste instead of the ship itself?

- Why did Dr. Ballard use a robot to explore the wreck?

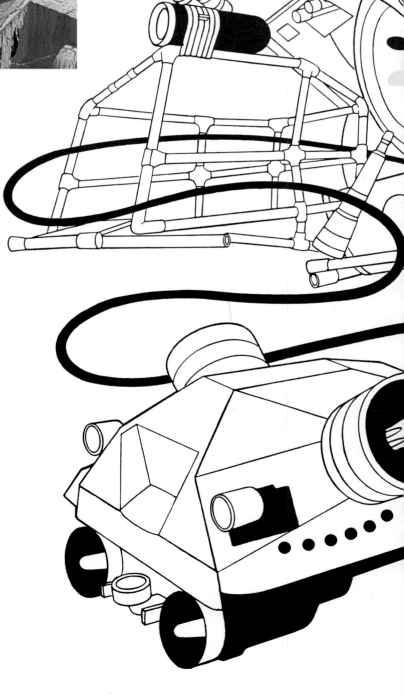

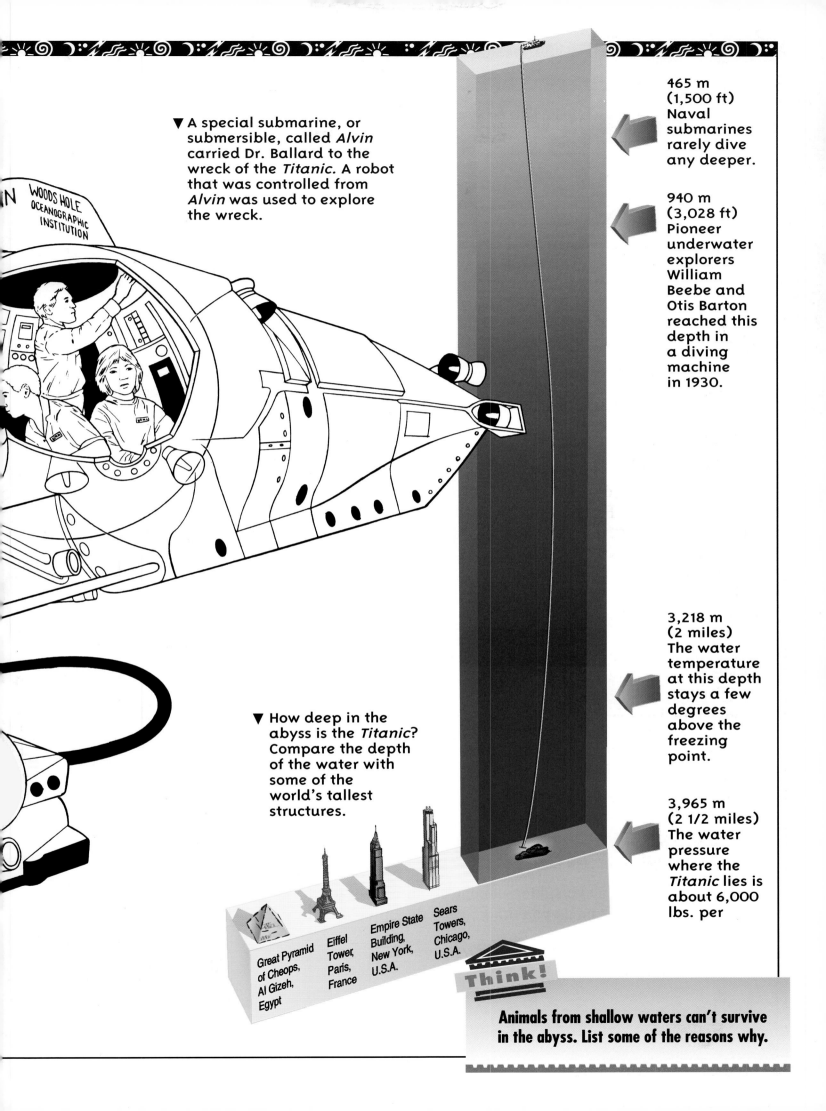

▼ A special submarine, or submersible, called *Alvin* carried Dr. Ballard to the wreck of the *Titanic*. A robot that was controlled from *Alvin* was used to explore the wreck.

WOODS HOLE OCEANOGRAPHIC INSTITUTION

465 m (1,500 ft) Naval submarines rarely dive any deeper.

940 m (3,028 ft) Pioneer underwater explorers William Beebe and Otis Barton reached this depth in a diving machine in 1930.

▼ How deep in the abyss is the *Titanic*? Compare the depth of the water with some of the world's tallest structures.

3,218 m (2 miles) The water temperature at this depth stays a few degrees above the freezing point.

3,965 m (2 1/2 miles) The water pressure where the *Titanic* lies is about 6,000 lbs. per

Great Pyramid of Cheops, Al Gizeh, Egypt

Eiffel Tower, Paris, France

Empire State Building, New York, U.S.A.

Sears Towers, Chicago, U.S.A.

Think!

Animals from shallow waters can't survive in the abyss. List some of the reasons why.

What Lives at the Surface?

You've learned about many ocean organisms: the strange fishes of the abyss, mammals that roam the open ocean, the beautiful corals of the continental shelf, and many others. The huge blue whale and the small coral animal both depend on something else for food: <u>plankton</u>. Plankton are microscopic organisms that float and drift by the billions near the surface of the ocean. Most living things on land—including you—depend on plankton, too.

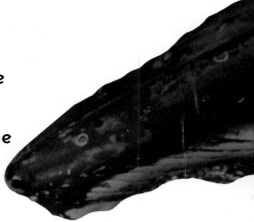

Exploration:
Observe plankton.

You need:
Plankton sample
Hand lens
Dish

❶ Use a hand lens to observe the plankton in the sample. Are they all similar? Draw a picture of one of the organisms.

❷ Now look at the photograph on this page. It shows another kind of plankton, hundreds of times larger than its actual size. How does this kind of plankton compare with the plankton you observed in the sample?

▼ *Oscillatoria*, a kind of plankton.

Interpret your results.

• There are two main kinds of plankton: <u>zooplankton</u>—which are animals or animal-like plankton, and <u>phytoplankton</u>—which are a little like plants. Which kind was the plankton in the sample? Explain.

• Which of the two planktons you observed do you think is larger in real life?

• One of the kinds of plankton depends on the other to survive. Which one do you think needs the other? Why?

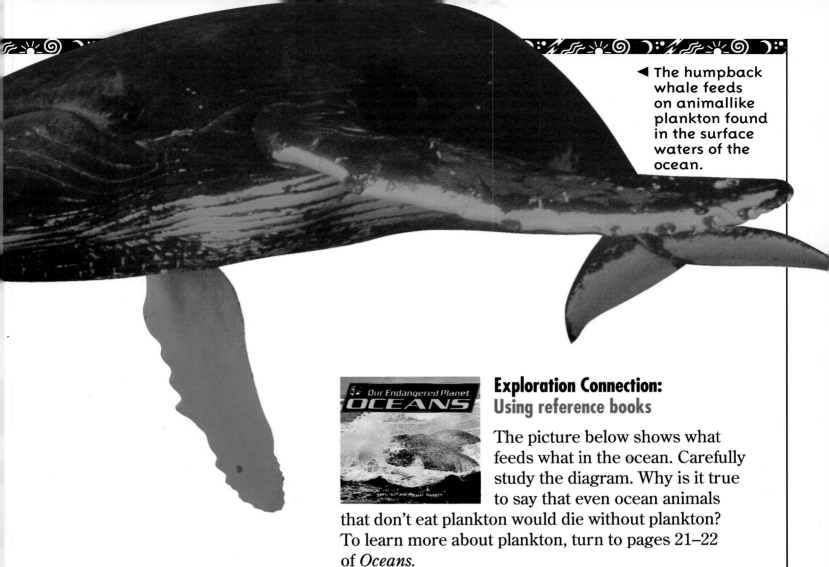

◀ The humpback whale feeds on animallike plankton found in the surface waters of the ocean.

Exploration Connection:
Using reference books

The picture below shows what feeds what in the ocean. Carefully study the diagram. Why is it true to say that even ocean animals that don't eat plankton would die without plankton? To learn more about plankton, turn to pages 21–22 of *Oceans*.

WHAT FEEDS WHAT?

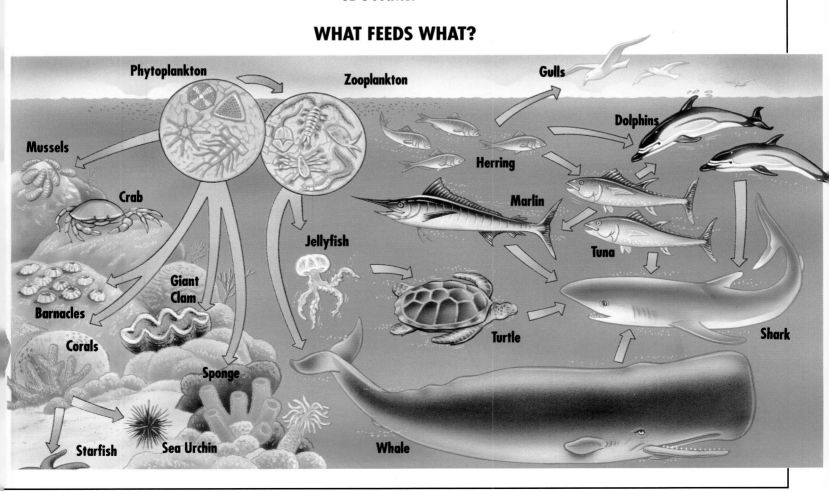

Phytoplankton   Zooplankton   Gulls

Mussels   Crab   Dolphins

Herring   Marlin   Tuna

Jellyfish   Barnacles   Giant Clam

Corals   Sponge   Turtle   Shark

Starfish   Sea Urchin   Whale

Blue whales can grow to be over 30 meters (100 feet) long. How do you think such a huge animal collects tiny plankton to eat? Compare the blue whale's mouth with the orca's mouth. What differences do you notice in their mouth parts? Many animals eat plankton. They all have special ways to catch them.

Exploration:
Make a baleen model.

You need:
Paint tray
Water
Tiny scraps of paper
Plastic bottle
Comb

❶ Fill the tray with water. Scatter the paper scraps in it. The scraps of paper represent plankton.

❷ Fill the bottle with water by holding its opening in the tray and squeezing the bottle. The bottle represents a blue whale's mouth.

❸ How can you use the comb to filter the scraps of paper out of the water? Try it. Record your results. ✎

Interpret your results.

• Look at the mouth of the blue whale. What mouth parts does the comb represent?

• How is the comb different from the mouth parts of the orca?

• How does a blue whale catch plankton?

◄ Observe the teeth of this orca, or killer whale. What kind of food do you think it eats?

► Instead of teeth, blue whales have baleen. It hangs in long strips from the whale's upper jaw, and it's made of the same kind of material as your fingernails.

Closer to Home:
The air you breathe

Used up any oxygen lately? Even when you're sitting still, you breathe about 15 times a minute—and so does every other human in the world. Nearly all other kinds of living things take in oxygen every minute, day and night. Why doesn't the oxygen in the air get used up?

You can thank phytoplankton for about half of the oxygen in the air. Phytoplankton put together carbon dioxide gas, sunlight, and water to make sugar, the food they need. During this process, they also make oxygen. Phytoplankton don't need most of the oxygen they make. Instead, they release the extra oxygen into the water. Plankton floating near the surface of the ocean make about half of all the oxygen in the air.

- How do you think oxygen gets from the water into the air?

- If most of the plankton in the ocean were destroyed, how would it affect other living things in the ocean?

- How would this disaster affect you and everything else that lives on land?

Think!

Which organisms have a greater effect on ocean life— plankton, fish, or whales? Explain your answer.

How Does the Ocean Feed People?

Knowing that tiny phytoplankton affect every breath you take makes you realize just how important plankton are, doesn't it? They're important to you in another way if you eat seafood. If you eat sardines, smelt, or herring, you eat fish that eat zooplankton. Tuna feed on sardines, smelt, and herring. Without zooplankton, all of those fish—and most others—would die.

Many food fish swim in large groups called schools or shoals. A smelt school, for example, can include millions of smelt. People on fishing boats search for these huge schools with sonar, the same machine people who map the ocean floor use.

A sonar machine sends out sound that travels through the water. When this sound hits an object, it bounces back to the ship. If an object is above the ocean floor, some of the sound bounces off the object before the rest of the sound bounces off the ocean floor. If the object is big, it's probably a school of fish. The boat moves until it's above the school and then the crew drops its nets on the school.

Many fishing boats use huge nets. The diagram shows the size of the largest of these nets. Imagine how many fish could be caught in a net that size. How could catching so many fish at one time affect the ocean's food resources?

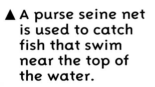

▲ A purse seine net is used to catch fish that swim near the top of the water.

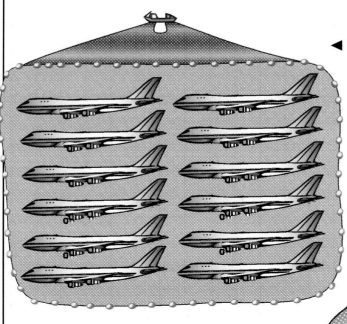

◄ The world's largest fishing net, a purse seine, could hold 12 jumbo jets.

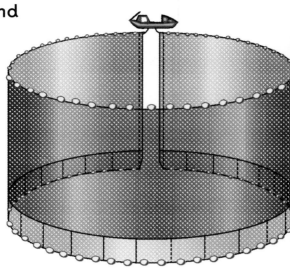

◄ An otter trawl net is dragged on the ocean floor to catch animals that live there.

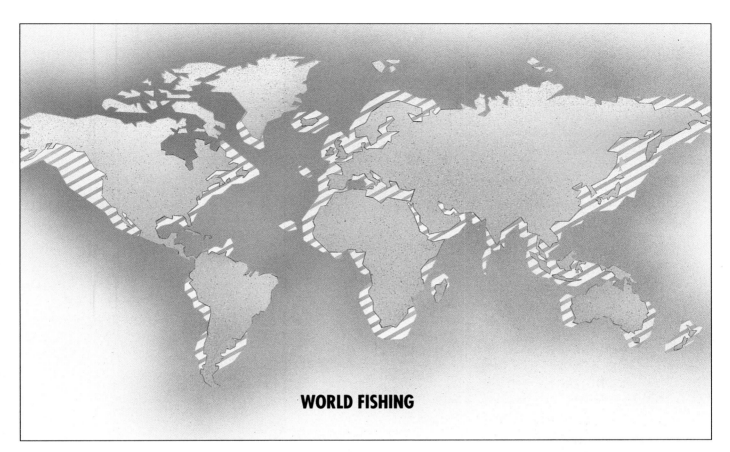

WORLD FISHING

▲ The areas in stripes show the most important fishing areas in the world.

Information Connection:
Using reference books

The map shows some of the most important fishing areas in the world. What part of the ocean are most of these areas in—the water above the continental shelf, the open ocean, or the abyss?

More people around the world are fishing today than ever before, especially for large fish like tuna. The graph shows the amount of bluefin tuna caught in the Atlantic Ocean between 1970 and 1990. What do the bars show? How would you explain the changes?

To find out which countries are doing the most ocean fishing, turn to pages 25 and 26 of *Oceans*.

BLUEFIN TUNA CATCH

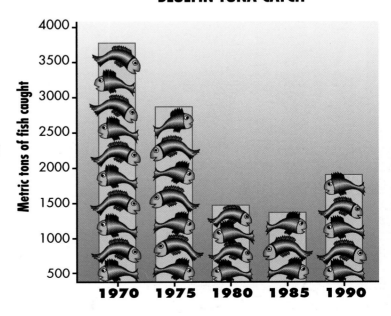

Closer to Home:
Ocean groceries

Even if you don't eat fish or shrimp or clams or any of the other ocean animals people catch and eat, you still eat food from the ocean. In fact, if you go to some of America's biggest hamburger chains and order a low-fat hamburger, you'll eat seafood!

The meat on that hamburger is part beef and part carrageen. Carrageen comes from a few kinds of seaweed. Some of this seaweed is grown on farms like the one in the picture. Carrageen is used in the products shown.

Sea farms may become one of the best sources of food for people—and not just seaweed farms. Right now, about one-tenth of the fish that people eat are raised on fish farms. Clams, oysters, shrimp, and lobsters are also raised in sea farms.

- How do you think the work of a sea farmer is like the work of a land farmer? How is it different?

- How might sea farming help solve the problem shown on the bar graph on page 47?

▼ Seaweed is in many of the products you use.

Jelly

Fluoride
Mint Toothpaste
NET WT 6.4 OZ (181 g)

▲ Seaweed can be raised on farms in the ocean.

Think!

Sonar and big nets have helped and hurt people who fish for a living. Explain.

What Other Ocean Resources Do People Use?

In many parts of the world, people depend on the ocean to supply them with food. However, food is just one ocean resource that people use. Salt is another one. Even diamonds are found in the ocean! Diamonds are mined from the ocean floor off the coast of Africa. There are tiny amounts of metals dissolved in ocean water. The pictures below show manganese nodules—lumps of metal that form on the floor of the abyss. Manganese is a metal used in making steel, glass, and batteries.

Exploration:
Observe a sea-floor nodule.

You need:

Centimeter ruler
Hand lens
Pencil
Paper

❶ Observe the pictures of a manganese nodule with your hand lens. Describe the nodule. ✎

❷ A nodule forms as metal collects around a small object such as a pebble or a shark's tooth. Scientists think that these layers increase by about 1 millimeter every 500,000 years. How could you figure out the age of the nodule in the pictures?

❸ Do you think that the nodules were formed by more than one kind of metal? What makes you think that? Draw what you think the nodule looked like when it was half as old as it is. ✎

► Manganese nodule, outside (actual size)

▼ Manganese nodule, inside (actual size)

Interpret your results.

• Manganese nodules also contain copper and other valuable metals. But getting the nodules out of the ocean costs too much. Can you think of reasons why?

• Where does the metal that forms in layers around a nodule come from?

• What do you think would have to happen to make collecting the nodules less costly?

Exploration Connection:
Using reference books

Manganese nodules lie on the ocean floor. Petroleum, another ocean resource, is found in the rock that forms the ocean floor. Wells are drilled into the ocean floor to reach the petroleum. Gasoline, plastic, and many other things are made from petroleum.

The map shows where most of the offshore oil wells around the United States are located. Compare this map with the one on pages 28–29. Are most of the wells on the continental shelf or in the open ocean?

The picture shows the equipment at the top of an ocean oil well. Sometimes these wells leak oil into the water. Also, ships that carry oil from place to place sometimes get caught in storms and dump oil into the ocean. To learn about the effects of oil spills, turn to pages 41–43 and 56–58 of *Oceans*.

▲ Top of an ocean oil well

U.S. OFFSHORE OIL WELLS

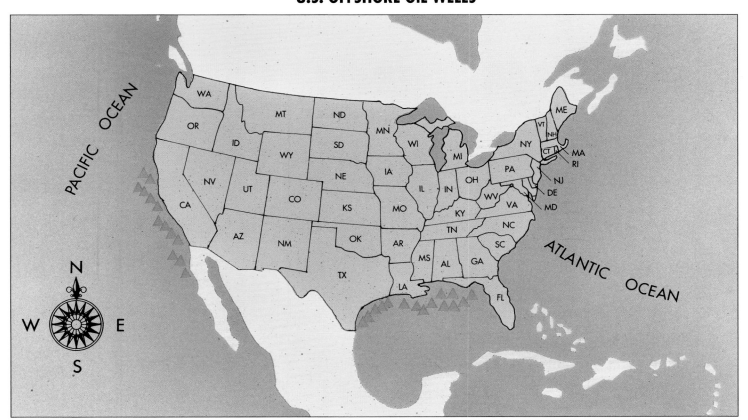

▲ This map shows where offshore drilling for petroleum takes place near the United States.

So far, you've learned about several resources found in or under the ocean. Food resources live in the ocean. Minerals can be taken out of the water or found lying on the ocean floor. Oil comes from under the ocean floor. What about the water itself? How do you think ocean water can be used as a resource?

Exploration:
Make a solar still.

You need:
Clear plastic cup
Black paper
Tape
Water
Salt
Dish
Plastic bag

❶ Wrap black paper around a cup and tape it in place.

❷ Fill the cup three-fourths full of water. Add some salt to the water and stir until the salt dissolves.

❸ Place the dish in a sunny spot. Place the cup in the dish. Put the plastic bag over the dish and cup. Tape the bag to the dish.

❹ Wait three hours. Observe the plastic and the dish.

▶ Every bit of space on a cargo ship is filled—even the deck.

Interpret your results.

• How do you think the water inside and outside the cup differs? How could you find out?

• Why did you need sunlight and black paper? How could you find out? **Try it!**

• What resource does a solar still take from the ocean? How do people use this resource?

Closer to Home:
Ocean roads

Ocean water is used in another way. There are probably many things in your classroom that came from places on other continents. How did they get to your classroom? Products are carried across the ocean in two ways—by ship or by plane.

Oil tankers are just one kind of ship that carries a product. In fact, nearly everything that comes to the United States from other continents is brought here by ship—and vice versa. Ships can carry huge amounts of cargo. The largest ships can haul about 500,000 metric tons. That's as much as 50,000 school buses would weigh!

Cargo ships carry all kinds of products. They haul unfinished materials such as wood, rubber, and metal ores. Do you eat bananas? Like many fruits and vegetables, they travel by ship to reach the United States. So do cars, machinery, televisions, and many other products. Check the labels on your clothing. If something you're wearing was made outside North America, it probably took a long ride in a big ship.

- Airplanes are faster than ships. Why do ships—not airplanes—carry most products to the United States?

- Most big cities are on the coast. Why do people build cities on the coast?

Think!

Why is it so important to take care of the ocean?

How Else Do People Change the Ocean?

Any time people use an ocean resource, they change the ocean in some way. Taking salt out of ocean water changes the water. Drilling an oil well into the ocean floor changes the floor. Some changes, such as oil spills, are accidents. It's easy to see how an accident can be harmful. But changes that are made on purpose can be harmful, too. Building sea walls is one such change. Sea walls are built to protect beaches. That sounds like a good idea, doesn't it? The picture shows sea walls along a stretch of beach. What kinds of changes do you think can happen when people build sea walls?

Exploration:
Build a sea-wall model.

You need:
Paint tray
Sand
Rocks
Water
Straw

❶ Make a model beach by putting about 2.5 centimeters (1 inch) of sand in the raised end of the tray. Pour water into the deep end of the tray until it reaches your beach.

❷ Use the rocks to build a model sea wall from the beach out into the water, as shown in the pictures. How do you think the sea wall will affect the beach and the ocean floor? ✏

❸ Working from the side of the tray, blow through the straw on the surface of the water like the person in the picture is doing. Blow several times and observe what happens. ✏

Interpret your results.

• When you blew across the water, how did the rocks affect what happened?

• How do sea walls change beaches?

▲ Sea walls are built to keep beach sand from moving along the coast.

Exploration Connection: Using reference books

Many of the ways people change the ocean cause other changes that nobody thought would happen. Some of the worst changes happen to the ocean's life. The Kemp's ridley sea turtle is a good example. In 1945, there were about 40,000 female Kemp's ridleys in the ocean. Look at the graph. About how many females were alive in 1975? What do you think happened between 1945 and 1975 to cause this change?

What change happened between 1985 and 1990? What might be the reasons for this change? To find out more about how human changes have harmed ocean life, read "Belly Up in the Bay" on pages 49–51 of *Oceans*.

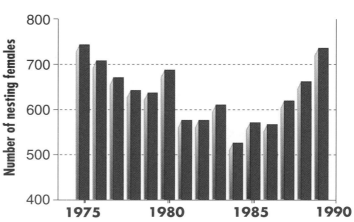

▶ Baby Kemp's ridley sea turtle

FEMALE KEMP'S RIDLEY SEA TURTLE POPULATION

Number of nesting females

800
700
600
500
400

1975   1980   1985   1990

Sometimes human actions that happen far from the ocean can cause changes in the ocean. These changes can also harm other living things besides the ones in the ocean.

Exploration:
Connect land and water.

You need:

Paint tray
Sand
Medicine dropper
Blue food dye
Cup
Water

❶ Cover most of the bottom of the tray with damp sand. Pour water into the deepest end of the tray to represent the ocean.

❷ The shallow end of the tray represents farms far from the ocean. Farmers use chemicals on their fields. Put two or three drops of food dye on the sand at the shallow end of your tray.

❸ Slowly pour a cup of water on the sand near the dye. The water represents rain. Observe what happens for ten minutes.

Interpret your results.

• What happened to the dye?

• How do farm chemicals get into the ocean?

• How could the chemicals affect fish and other ocean life?

• How could the chemicals affect people?

▼ Using the ocean as a garbage dump harms many ocean creatures.

▼ This bird is caught in the plastic rings from a six-pack of soda.

Closer to Home: Plastic trash

Farm chemicals aren't the only pollution that travels to the ocean from far away. Does your family buy soda in six-packs? What do you do with the plastic ring when the last can is gone? That plastic ring could easily end up in the ocean. So could empty plastic bread bags, dry-cleaning bags, and garbage bags.

Have you ever watched hundreds of small gas-filled balloons go up into the air? It's a beautiful sight, but what goes up must come down. Many of those balloons travel for hundreds of miles and then fall into the ocean.

A plastic six-pack ring can get caught around an animal's neck and can choke the animal. This often happens to seagulls and young seals. A floating balloon or plastic bag looks like a jellyfish. Many whales, sea turtles, and other animals eat jellyfish. Many dead sea turtles and whales have been found with plastic bags in their stomachs or intestines. The bags killed the animals.

Plastic trash is a big problem, especially in cities that send their trash by train or truck to the ocean. Hopefully, we'll find better ways to get rid of our trash than dumping it in the ocean.

- You might not be able to stop cities from dumping trash in the ocean right now, but how can you make your trash a little safer?

Think!

How could garbage dumped from a ship in the open ocean pollute a beach?

Identify Problems: Living Under Water

Think Tank Road-Map

More than five billion people live on our planet. Finding enough food to feed them and enough land for everyone to live on is one of the biggest problems of the 21st century. You and your team of explorers believe that the answer to a modern problem may just be where life first began – in the ocean.

15 • In Lesson 15, you'll identify problems you'll have to solve in order to live in the ocean for two months.

16 • In Lesson 16, you'll identify some possible solutions to these problems.

17 • In Lesson 17, you'll design an underwater habitat. Then you'll make a model based on your design.

 You may also want to review the video.

Problem: Your team's job is to plan and build an underwater habitat. It will have to be big enough for your class to live in for two months. Your habitat will be the first step in a worldwide project to build cities in the ocean.

These questions will help you make a list of the problems you'll face while trying to design an underwater habitat:

1 What have you already learned about the ocean that could cause problems for people who want to build and live in an underwater habitat?

2 How many people will you be living with? What will all of you need to stay alive underwater?

3 Which of the things you need can come from the ocean? How will you get them? Which will you have to take with you?

4 What jobs will have to be done in order to maintain the habitat?

5 You aren't the first people to go into an environment that's hard for people to live in. The explorers on these pages faced challenges, too. Study each picture and ask yourself: What problems did these explorers have to solve?

◀ **Space shuttle** Astronauts need special equipment to survive in space. They can live and work for several days in a space shuttle. How is living in a space shuttle like living in an underwater habitat?

▶ **Desert hike** Deserts can have very extreme temperatures. What would a team of explorers who went backpacking in the desert for a week need to know about their environment? How is surviving in a desert like living in an ocean?

◀ **Antarctica research camp** Antarctica is the coldest place on Earth. How can scientists make discoveries in an icy environment like this? What problems do they have to solve in order to live and work where it's so cold? How are their problems like yours?

Think!

Of the three explorations shown, which has problems most like those facing your team? How?

Finding Solutions: Living Under Water

What's an oceanographer, anyway?

Data in the Exploration Connections was gathered by oceanographers, scientists who study the ocean. Physical oceanographers study waves, tides, currents, and the atmosphere. Chemical oceanographers study the chemical reactions in seawater, and marine biologist study marine life. Ocean engineers design the research tools and machinery for much of this ocean exploration.

▲ Spacesuits
Astronauts work outside the shuttle in spacesuits. A special rocket-powered backpack helps astronauts move around.

You just identified some problems explorers of other environments faced. Now you'll take a closer look at one of them — the space shuttle. A team of scientists worked together to design a shuttle that would blast off like a rocket, land like an airplane, and keep several astronauts alive in space. Studying their solutions to living in space might help you and your team of oceanographers find solutions for living under water.

1

Make a chart of the problems you listed in the last lesson. Beside each problem, try to list a similar problem the shuttle crew has to deal with. You might not be able to think of a matching problem.

2

Study the diagram of the space shuttle. Do these solutions give you new ideas for solving your problems? Below each shuttle problem on your chart, record any solutions that you find.

3

Study the photo of the astronaut. How does special equipment help solve the shuttle crew's problems?

4

Below each of the living underwater problems on your chart, record any solutions you can think of. If you have more than one solution to a problem, record them. Use both words and pictures.

SPACE SHUTTLE DESIGN

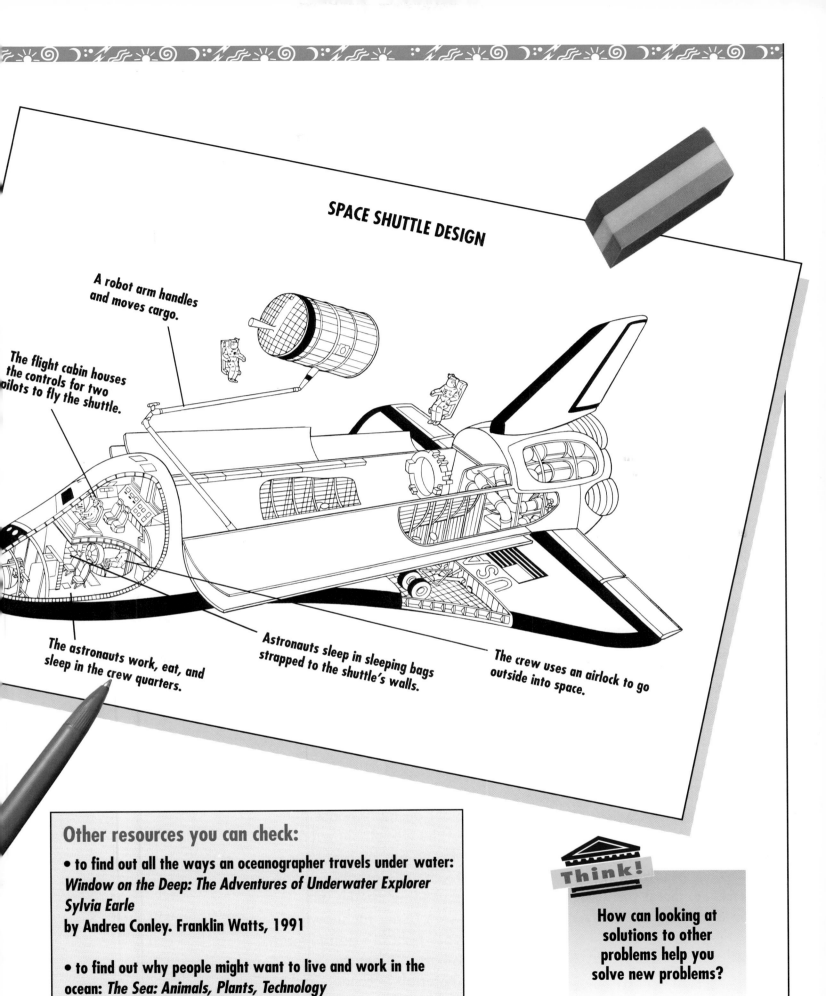

A robot arm handles and moves cargo.

The flight cabin houses the controls for two pilots to fly the shuttle.

The astronauts work, eat, and sleep in the crew quarters.

Astronauts sleep in sleeping bags strapped to the shuttle's walls.

The crew uses an airlock to go outside into space.

Other resources you can check:

• to find out all the ways an oceanographer travels under water: *Window on the Deep: The Adventures of Underwater Explorer Sylvia Earle* by Andrea Conley. Franklin Watts, 1991

• to find out why people might want to live and work in the ocean: *The Sea: Animals, Plants, Technology* by Brian Williams. Kingfisher Books, 1991

Think!

How can looking at solutions to other problems help you solve new problems?

Make Models: Living Under Water

Possible models for your habitat:

Diagram Use the diagrams in Lessons 6, 10, and 16 to help you draw a large diagram of your underwater habitat. Be sure to label the diagram to show your solutions.

3-Dimensional Model Use clay, cardboard, or any combination of materials to build a model of your underwater habitat.

Written Description Write a report that carefully describes every detail of your habitat: its parts, its size, its materials, and so on.

Computer Graphics Use a graphics program to design an underwater habitat on the computer.

Interview Tape-record a description of your under water habitat as though your team were giving an interview to a news reporter.

Your team has identified problems you'll face in living under water. You've also identified possible solutions to some of those problems. Now it's time to put those solutions to work.

1

Look through your *Student's Map* for a picture that shows a good site for your underwater habitat. Does your choice create new problems that you'll have to solve?

2

Work with your team to design an underwater habitat. List all the things your habitat should have. Make sure your design includes these things.

3

Make a model based on your design. Choose one of the models shown on this page. You and your team will probably decide that some models will work better for showing your habitat's design than others. Gather the materials you need and start working.

4

Look at all the models your class has made. How did different teams solve problems? Did everybody think of the same problems? the same solutions?

5

How would your models have been different if you hadn't learned about water pressure in this unit? about currents? What were the most important things that you learned in this unit that helped you design an underwater habitat?

Resources for designing your habitat:

• Your own journals or your Labmats from the Explorations in the unit are filled with valuable data you've collected and conclusions you've made about the ocean.

• Look back at the graphics and information in Lessons 1-14 of *Student's Map to Exploration.*

• The two reference books you've used all through this unit are filled with lots of additional information about ocean exploration.

• Refer to the Video Clue Log. What ocean characteristics did the Science Sleuths investigate? Which of these might you consider when designing your habitat?

• You can interview members of another team and offer to trade information with them.

How did making a model help you think of problems and solutions you missed before?

FOR SCIENCE BROWSERS

All articles reprinted with permission.

Sea Spiders
by *Cathy Walsh*
from *Ranger Rick*

Even with their long legs, *sea spiders* will never win any ocean marathons. These animals are creepy, crawly, and slow...slow... s-l-o-w.

Sea spiders poke along in all the world's oceans. Most of the 900 *species* (kinds) are pretty small. Two or three of the smallest could sit side-by-side on top of a thumbtack. But the ones that live in the coldest oceans are much bigger. The biggest sea spider ever found measured 30 inches (75 cm) from leg tip to leg tip.

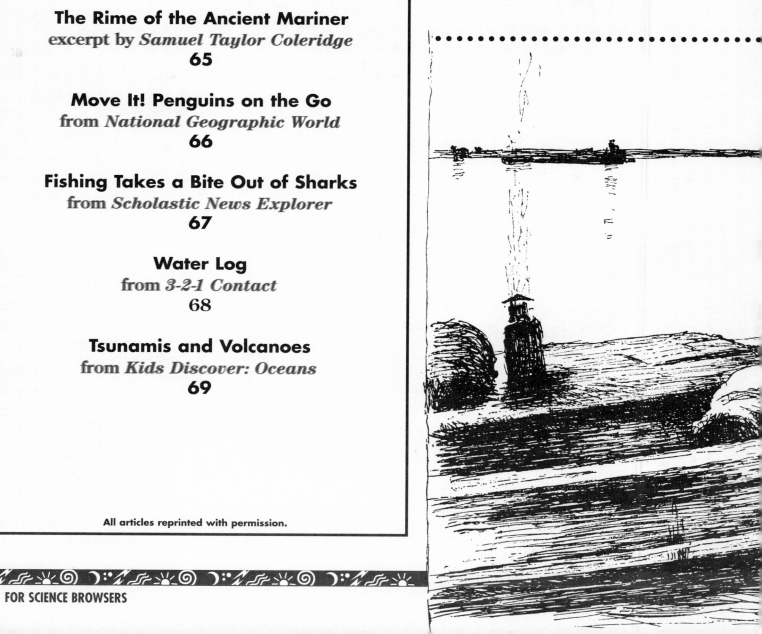

Crawly Cousins

Sea spiders aren't really spiders. They're related to spiders and have eight legs, as spiders do. But spiders have bigger bodies than sea spiders. A sea spider's body has very little room inside it. So the sea spider's intestines and sex organs are in its legs!

Unlike most of their spider cousins, sea spiders don't build webs. So how do they catch food? Well, the only food a sea spider can "catch" is food that stays still.

A sea spider crawls along looking for corals, anemones, sponges, and other animals that live attached to

©NHPA/Agence Nature

things. When it finds something to eat, it stabs the animal with its *proboscis* (pro-BAH-sis). Using this long, skinny mouthpart like a straw, the sea spider slurps up the animal's body juices. — *August, 1993* ◉

The Rime of the Ancient Mariner

excerpt by
Samuel Taylor Coleridge

All in a hot and copper sky,
The bloody Sun, at noon,
Right up above the mast did stand,
No bigger than the Moon.

Day after day, day after day,
We stuck, nor breath, nor motion;
As idle as a painted ship
Upon a painted ocean.

Water, water everywhere
And all the boards did shrink;
Water, water everywhere,
Nor any drop to drink

Bubble Net

Fishing with a net of bubbles sounds like an unlikely way to catch anything. Humpback whales have perfected the technique. Spotting a school of fish, a humpback swims beneath it in a circle, releasing a stream of air bubbles. The school is surrounded by a "net" of bubbles. The fish could swim through the bubbles, but they seem confused. The humpback can then easily gulp down its prey.

Move It! Penguins on the Go

by *Charles Norlandea*

©Tom Brakefield/Stock Market

Mudskipper

The mudskipper fish can climb up a mangrove tree. It hangs from a branch and waits for the tide to come in. Its large eyes swivel in all directions—even backwards!

Hatchery

The male seahorse carries the fertilized eggs in a "breed pouch" until they hatch!

Penguins may look slow and clumsy, but that's because people usually see them on land. Their bullet-shaped bodies are best suited to the place where they spend the most time: the sea. Penguins are super swimmers. With feet tucked back and necks stretched out, they slip easily through the water. They propel themselves with powerful flippers, and steer with their feet and tail.

Millions of these unique birds live in the icy regions of **Antarctica,** so it's not surprising they've developed some unique ways of getting around.

One of their slickest moves, shown above, is called porpoising. For a few brief seconds penguins look like porpoises and appear to be flying! What they're really doing is filling their lungs with air. Penguins push themselves out of the sea with their flippers in order to breathe, then reenter the water without losing any speed. The total "flight" covers a distance two or three times their body length.

Climbing out of the sea onto an icy ledge can present a slippery challenge. Adélie penguins solve that problem with a jazzy jump that rockets them from the water directly onto the ice. Once again, it's flipper power that provides the push.

Even on land, penguins can move quickly. They're slow starters, but penguins can run at a good clip once they get going. And when they *really* need to hurry, penguins flop down and "toboggan." By sliding on their bellies and pushing with flippers and feet, they can zoom across snow and ice.

So remember, looks can be deceiving. For birds that can't fly, penguins sure know how to get around. — *December, 1993* ◉

©Francsco Erizo/Bruce Coleman

Fishing Takes A Bite Out Of Sharks

by *John Shabe*
from *Scholastic News Explorer*

When kids swim in the ocean, some are afraid of being eaten by a shark. But it is far more likely that a shark will be eaten by one of them. In fact, humans' big appetite is putting some shark species in danger.

In 1989, fishers caught 8,000 tons of shark. That is about 50 times more than the amount caught in 1979. Most of those sharks were sold to restaurants and fish markets.

Shark Protection

The U.S. government is working on a new law to protect sharks. The new law would set limits on how many sharks fishers are allowed to catch. Last year, hundreds of people wrote the government, asking for a law to protect sharks.

"Right now, fishers can kill as many sharks as they want," said Sonja Fordham of the Center for Marine Conservation. The Center tries to protect undersea creatures. "We want some basic limits on how many sharks they can catch."

Why Save Sharks?

Experts say saving sharks will help everyone. Sharks are an important part of sea life. They help nature keep a balance underwater by eating certain sea creatures.

For example, sharks near Florida often eat fish called stingrays. But now, because there are fewer sharks, there are more stingrays. A stingray's sharp tail can give a swimmer a painful wound. And all those stingrays are eating a lot of small fish. Experts think they may be eating too many.

How Many Sharks Are Left?

Even experts are not sure exactly how many sharks are left in the world's oceans. Because sharks roam huge areas of ocean, they are hard to count. But shark watchers say there are fewer sharks these days. Scientist Samuel Gruber said

©Ron and Valerie Taylor/Bruce Coleman

he used to study lemon sharks in the ocean near Florida. But he doesn't any more. He can't find enough lemon sharks to study.

Experts say it is important for the U.S. government to make laws to protect sharks. Soon it may be too late to save some sharks from becoming extinct. — *April, 1993*

Fresh Water

More than 100 million gallons of sea water a day are converted into fresh water throughout the world.

Garbage

Every year about nine million tons of garbage sludge are dumped into the ocean off the coast of New York City.

Water Log

by *Karen Romano Young*
from *3–2–1 Contact*

Jon Hoech was a kid who loved fish. He kept home aquariums. And when he was in high school, he ran a pet store that sold fish tanks and supplies. He studied biology in college, then got a job at the Monterey Bay Aquarium, in Monterey, CA. You should see his fish tanks now!

One is the world's tallest fish tank—28 feet deep. It houses giant kelp plants, leopard sharks, sea urchins and sardines. There's the Monterey Bay habitats exhibit, which is as long as three school buses. It's chock full of sharks, bat rays, striped bass and hundreds of other creatures.

Hoech (say: *hosh*) is an aquarist. His job is to keep the tanks clean, beautiful, healthy and full. That's pretty simple to do for a home aquarium. But for a large public aquarium—a kind of zoo for fish—it takes a lot of work.

Fit Fish

"The first thing I do when I get here in the morning is to look things over," Hoech says. "I check to see that the fish and animals look healthy and normal."

Monterey Bay Aquarium has an open water system. That means fresh seawater is pumped into the tanks.

The water brings in tiny fish, eggs and spores that grow into plants. "When something grows too big for the tank, we let it go back in the ocean."

Spooge Alert!

Next it's housecleaning time. "I play around with the rocks and gravel on the bottom of the tank. They get moved by the animals and by water currents. I rearrange them so they'll look their best."

It won't matter how pretty they look if the glass tank is covered with slimy algae: Visitors won't be able to see anything. "Under the sea, algae naturally covers rocks and walls," Hoech explains. "It's a big job to keep the windows clear." The job is so big that Monterey Bay's aquarists have made up their own word for the gooey slime that covers walls and clogs filters: spooge.

Aquarists working in small tanks can attach a nylon sponge to a pole and scrape algae from the windows. For heavy-duty jobs, Hoech dons a wet suit and dives in the tank where the large octopus lives.

Feeding Time

Small creatures eat the algae and spores. Larger fish eat chunks of food that aquarists pour into the tanks. To hand-feed leopard sharks and big fish, Hoech puts chunks of fish on the end of a bamboo pole. He does this to keep track of who eats what. It also discourages animals from competing for food.

Doesn't feeding sharks by hand make Hoech a little nervous? "I've never felt like I was in danger," he states. "Sharks will give me the eye, but they don't really follow me. I watch to make sure that no large animal is showing any aggression—swimming toward me or circling quickly. It hasn't happened yet." This is one reason for keeping careful feeding records: Hoech doesn't want any hungry hunters in his tanks! — *November, 1993* ✪

©1994 Rick Browne/Monterey Bay Aquarium

Tsunamis And Volcanoes
from *Kids Discover: Oceans*

When an earthquake originates deep inside the earth, the waves go through water as well as land. When these waves (tsunamis) hit the shore, they often do more damage than the quake alone does.

Volcanic eruptions can come with earthquakes, too, but more often under the ocean than on land. Deep trenches are formed on the ocean floor when plates push against each other and one is forced under the other, causing an earthquake. Some of the molten rock that lies under the earth's crust then pushes up and out, causing an eruption.

When one plate is forced below another, the process is called subduction. Subduction pulls some of the earth's crust into the mantle. In turn some of the soft, hot rock in the mantle rises up and becomes crust.

Earthquakes can be deadly, but can they wipe an entire city from the face of the earth? Well, that's exactly what happened on the Mediterranean island of Cyprus in A.D. 365, and no one found out about it until 1934—over 1500 years later! The massive quake struck at dawn while most people were indoors. It was followed by a deadly tsunami, traveling at about 500 miles per hour. The thousands who lived in the city of Kourion and in other parts of Cyprus were never seen or heard from again. — *May, 1992* ✪

NOAA/EDIS

Giant Iceberg

The biggest iceberg ever seen had a bigger surface area than the country of Belgium.

Male or Female?

The sand perch, razorfish, and tilefish can all change from female to male! Some other fish, like the clownfish, make the opposite change, from male to female.

GLOSSARY

Concept vocabulary and other technical terms

abyss [ə·bis′]: The part of the ocean that is deeper than 2 kilometers (1 1/2 miles).

abyssal plain [ə·bis·əl plān]: A flat or gently sloping region of the ocean floor; usually below a depth of 3.5 kilometers (2 miles).

bedrock [bed′·rok]: The solid rock under the looser materials of the earth's surface.

compass rose [kum′·pəs rōz]: A symbol on a map that shows directions.

continental shelf [kon·tə·nen′·təl shelf]: The undersea ledge that forms the rim of a continent.

continental slope [kon·tə·nen′·təl slōp]: The steep slope between the continental shelf and the ocean floor.

coral [kôr′·əl]: Tiny sea animals that live in the shallow ocean and feed on zooplankton.

coral reef [kôr′·əl rēf]: A stony limestone ridge near the surface of the water formed by the skeletons of sea coral.

current [kər′·ənt]: The steady movement of the ocean's surface water in a certain direction; caused in part by winds.

echolocation [ek·ō·lō·kā′·shən]: A process for locating distant or unseen objects with sound waves reflected back to the source.

mid-oceanic ridge [mid·ō·shē·an′·ik rij]: A chain of underwater mountains found on the ocean floor.

open ocean [ō′·pən ō′·shən]: The area of the ocean far from land.

phytoplankton [fī′·tō·plank·tən]: Plankton that carry out photosynthesis.

plankton [plank′·tən]: Organisms that float or drift in the sea; most plankton are small.

pressure [presh′·ər]: The amount of force pushing against an object.

prevailing winds [pri·vā′·ling winds]: Constant winds that are caused by the earth's rotation.

relief map [ri·lēf′ map]: A map on which differences in height above sea level are shown by lines, colors, or 3-D materials.

salinity [sə·lin′·ə·tē]: The amount of salt in water.

sonar [sō′·när]: A device that locates underwater objects by sending out high-frequency sound waves and picking up their echoes with a microphone.

storm winds [stôrm winds]: Winds that travel with storms; caused by changes in air pressure.

wave [wāv]: A moving ridge or swell on the surface of water; most waves are caused by the wind.

zooplankton [zō′·ə·plank′·tən]: Animal or animalike plankton.

a	add, map	i	it, give	u	up, done
ā	ace, rate	ī	ice, write	yōō	fuse, few
â(r)	care, air	o	odd, hot	û(r)	burn, term
ä	palm, father	ō	open, so	ə	*a in above*
e	end, pet	ô	order, jaw		*e in sicke*
ē	equal, tree	ōō	pool, food		